HOW TO LEAD YOUR BUSINESS BEYOND TQM

Making World Class Performance a Reality

Michael E Joyce

FT
PITMAN
PUBLISHING

PITMAN PUBLISHING
128 Long Acre, London WC2E 9AN

A Division of Pearson Professional Limited

First published in Great Britain 1995

British Library Cataloguing in Publication Data
A CIP catalogue record for this book can be obtained
from the British Library.

ISBN 0 273 61081 3

1 3 5 7 9 10 8 6 4 2

Typeset by PanTek Arts, Maidstone, Kent.
Printed and bound in Great Britain by
Biddles Ltd, Guildford and King's Lynn

*The Publishers' policy is to use paper manufactured
from sustainable forests.*

HOW TO LEAD
YOUR BUSINESS
BEYOND TQM

CONTENTS

FIGURES

INTRODUCTION

All organisations have a strong desire to be successful, and to be recognised for this success by building a reputation for excellence in their sphere of activity. I say organisations because this desire is the same whether it's a commercial company, a charity, an educational establishment, a hospital, in the private or public sector, full-time, part-time or voluntary.

Most organisations do achieve some level of success and some level of recognition. However, not all can sustain it; not all continue to be successful by developing their own ways of meeting the ever-changing challenges of the future. Organisations that are able to sustain success and continue to enjoy recognition and high reputation for their products, services, value for money, flexibility and innovation are few and hard to find. Organisations that do achieve such reputation, both large and small, become household names, not necessarily worldwide but certainly within their own locality and industry, and achieve a status that is clearly head and shoulders above the rest.

- *Why do organisations find it so difficult to maintain success once they have achieved it?*

- *How is it that some organisations continue to be successful and build increasingly high reputations?*

- *What is total quality management anyway and what has it got to do with being world class?*

- *Is there something beyond TQM?*

- *Can all organisations achieve continuing success and build ever higher reputations in their particular fields?*

- *How do you make it happen?*

The objective of this book is to address these questions and in answering them provide a blueprint of the essential elements and ingredients of achieving world class performance, including total quality management and beyond.

A world class company does not necessarily have a worldwide reputation, nor necessarily have worldwide operations. What it does have is a quality of management and leadership, operating systems and a culture and environment that would make it successful wherever it was located and whatever it did.

This book aims to demystify the aura surrounding 'world class performance' and demonstrate that it can be achieved by any organisation, providing it has the will to develop the skills to make it happen. The key to achieving world class performance within an organisation is in those last three words, *making it happen*.

Achieving world class performance within an organisation is very active and participative on the part of everyone, from the chief executive to the most junior employee. At times it is very hard work, painstaking work and at times frustrating. But it is also very rewarding and enriching.

The following chapters aim to paint word pictures of the art of the possible in terms of achieving world class performance. Questionnaires and checklists will enable you to examine your organisation and find the right route for you. Action plans will guide you to start the change yourselves and sustain the improvements that will be required if you are to achieve truly world class performance.

Consultants and trainers cannot of themselves achieve lasting success within organisations. They must own the actions they take and carry them out for themselves.

Within the Warmbrook Consultancy it has always been our policy, whenever called in by a client to undertake a project, that we look for the earliest point to leave, having provided them with the skills, knowledge and resources to carry out the work for themselves. This book is no exception. In it, the reader will be taken along a well-trod path. They will be invited to examine themselves and their organisation to see how they match up already to the challenges ahead.

There is no right route to world class performance. However, there are a number of key foundations and elements that must be addressed, and satisfied, if the organisation it to have any chance of achieving world class performance, or something like it, and a growing reputation. Initially, preparation and planning is required.

Chapter 1 will help you focus on the development of your organisation's own vision of what constitutes world class performance within the organisation and the industry. To some, the decision to change the culture of an organisation must be based on objective evidence that it will work and each element must be justified for inclusion; to others there is a strong personal belief that it will work and the action to change needs no justification. To them the first step is an act of faith.

In the first chapter we will consider the elements and pressures for change and how to develop a cultural model for a world class organisation; taking into account the needs of the various stakeholders in the model for change. You will be invited to consider how you measure up by comparing initiatives you have introduced in recent times against the world class organisation model. Also, you are invited to complete a company health check which will give pointers to the key elements of a model. A guide to using survey questionnaires to determine other inputs to the model are also be included. One output from the health check, will be a pointer to the key elements of establishing a vision and to highlight the important areas for improvement and change.

After reading this first chapter, the organisation should be able to start developing a vision, for their particular situation, knowing all the internal and external pressures for change. Managers should have a clear vision of the structure and culture they desire to have at some time in the future. Around this vision must be placed a firm strategy that identifies the type of competitive advantage and reputation the organisation is seeking and describes clearly how this is to be achieved.

To be successful with your quest for change, an action plan must be developed taking into account all the key stages of implementing the vision. This must create the environment in which a world class culture of empowerment, communication, recognition, measurement and commitment can grow. This is an essential element in long-term success, making your programme more than this year's campaign.

Careful planning is vital. This involves setting targets and milestones; identifying resources and skills necessary to implementing the changes; and monitoring progress.

Examples of good plans and proformas to help with the establishment of your own long-term plans are provided in *chapter 2*.

Typically, the biggest barrier to progress in the development of a world class culture is the senior management team itself. From the chief executive downwards, role model behaviour must be demonstrated. Selecting the right management style for the organisation and one that will support and enhance the cultural change required is all important. *Chapter 3* looks at the vexed question of senior management behaviour. Through questionnaires, it helps the senior team to examine current behaviour and develop an inventory of role model behaviours that being a world class company requires. Such behaviour will establish the core values of the new culture firmly in everyday affairs.

In *chapter 4*, we turn our attention to preparing the rest of the senior and middle managers for the changes ahead. Whilst some of them, if not all, will have contributed to the model for world class performance, they may, not appreciate the effects it will have on the way the organisation operates – and perhaps more importantly on the way they operate. Cultural change is management-led. It is active and is dependent on belief for success. But it is very much a case of 'soil *and* seed'. The soil may be a fertile environment, but if the seed is not good quality (and in this instance I refer to the capability of the managers and supervisors to cope with change), then the culture produced will be poor quality. So in chapter 4 we explore personal development, in particular the responsibilities of leadership; how power is exercised; getting the best from individuals; communicating with working groups; achieving tasks, and improving individual staff performance.

One of the biggest changes, particularly for middle managers and supervisors, is the role change from 'cop' to 'coach' and we will deal with the new skill of coaching. Once again, a series of checklists are provided to make quantitative and qualitative assessments of management style and provide a framework in which to launch the programme of change. Demonstrating role model behaviour in itself will not be entirely successful in achieving the changes required. Personal development, structures and the management and supervisory roles that the changes in culture and operation will bring about must also be addressed and planned before communicating the aspirations and direction for the future to the whole organisation.

The final part of the planning and preparation phase is to plan the actual communication of the vision and the changes desired, to the organisation. This is a key activity in that it is the first step in the process of change and it therefore must attract active and participative support from all areas. The reader is taken through a number of simple methods of successfully communicating the plans for change in *chapter 5* and materials that can be copied and adapted to suit the individual organisation are also provided. Top-quality communication is essential and visibility of early successes is also important, if time is not to be lost at the start.

Once the change process has started, concerns move to maintaining momentum, leading the cultural change and improvements to operational processes. Further, those activities must be measured to give a clear view of progress being made. Getting everyone involved is not easy, but the activity of charting the key processes of a department or section and analysing them has proven to be one of the best methods, because it is active and involves managers as well. Here we will deal with the methodology of process mapping and process analysis, together with other easy tools such as team purpose analysis which when used in tandem can provide a good foundation in the early motivation of activity. Examples of good and bad practice, the benefits of process mapping and other uses of process flowcharts once they have been established are examined.

Avoiding false starts and avoiding activity traps, logjams and bottlenecks is the central core of the initial launch process. *Chapter 6* shows how to deal with these by involving everyone, especially in the solution building.

During the planning stage, particularly when forming the implementation plan, progress measurement must be addressed. But more than that, in establishing the key areas for early, management-led improvement projects, targets for improvement must be set, as well as milestones to measure progress, and individual measurements to be made.

Choosing people to motivate others, operating as facilitators throughout the organisation is discussed in detail. In general terms, a facilitator is needed for each group of 30 people within an organisation. This person acts as the banner carrier for the whole change programme, provides support and expertise, and generally acts as a sounding board for managers and employees alike. The particular characteristics and criteria of such individuals is outlined in the form of checklists once again.

Chapter 7 deals with the cascade of these measures into the organisation and the ways in which individuals throughout the organisation can be encouraged to measure and report on their own performance. Once the processes of a department have been analysed, data gathering and simple measurement will also be required to determine if any improvement is actually taking place. What to measure and how to collect data is discussed. Guidance and examples are provided to help set up performance measurement and systems of review. Where departmental processes interface with others, usually between customers and suppliers, performance measures can be established and regular reviews agreed. Examples of agreements between internal customers and suppliers will be given, together with ideas for their establishment.

Providing simple data displays also assists employee support and involvement. Sample subjects together with real examples are given.

With all this activity, even if you have managed to avoid the traps, how do you know if real progress is being made? One tried and trusted method of measuring overall improvement is through the development and application of a simple *cost of quality model*. *Chapter 10* is devoted almost entirely to this and how to use such a model to measure return on investment in terms of effort and money in creating the cultural changes desired.

Like all chapters, chapter 10 can stand alone in terms of the activities described and can be used to carry out the individual task should the reader so choose. It is however referred to in *chapter 7* on developing a measurement culture, as the establishment of simple performance measurement will provide the basis for data collection for the internal and external failure sections. Consistent data collection and standardisation is all important in the establishment and maintenance of a quality cost model. The dangers of using such a device as anything more than a dipstick in measuring success will also be discussed.

Teamwork is one of the core practices in developing operational improvements and the reader will be introduced to the use of project teams, cross-functional teams and natural work teams in supporting the change process. Leading and managing these teams through a systematic process of examining tasks and activities, analysing them for opportunities for improvement and measuring their success is discussed and described in terms of best practice in *chapter 8*. Checklists are provided for potential leaders of these teams on team development, motivation and effective progress. Achieving this is a function of finding the right new role for middle managers and supervisors. The role is that of coach to the individuals and the teams.

The final element of implementing a culture change and creating a world class environment is a culture of continuous improvement. In *chapter 9* we will introduce methods of enabling staff in general to take direct action on failure to meet the standards set for both operations and core values. We will consider how to provide an internal customer complaints system and provision of the same levels of energy and resource to eliminate non-conforming situations, as is made available for external customer complaints.

An early problem described by many following this path, is that of losing good ideas and opportunities for improvement as they snowball from the early team projects. Developing a suitable system for capturing and monitoring these opportunities to improve the operation is vital and a number of good practices are described.

A huge number of organisations, big and small, have got off to a fast start. Yet many have nevertheless failed to reap the benefits of moving to change their cultures. Maintaining early momentum and converting early experiences into *business as usual* is the goal. Continuous improvement is not just problem-solving and making small improvements to processes, which in the main should have been done long before. Asking 'is there a better way?' plays a key role as does the powerful tool 'breakthrough thinking'. The effective use of breakthrough thinking requires considerable practice and, in the initial stages, a strong nerve to try some of the ideas.

Up to this point in the book we have been dealing with established ideas. Perhaps using some of the suggestions you can be more effective than many organisations with the implementation of what are really just common sense ideas. But if you are to be truly world class there is some thing else you must do.

You must develop a clear *business philosophy*. Having a clear vision of where you are headed (your mission) is not enough to achieve world class performance on its own. You need to specify the type of organisation you wish to become. You will need to develop a unique formula for meeting all of your stakeholders' requirements and provide a blueprint for all those in the organisation, now and in the future. A simple methodology to focus your attentions on the development of your business philosophy or *operating strategy* is described and discussed in *chapter 11*. It will enable you to specify 'the way we do things round here'.

Throughout the preceding chapters, a number of tools will have been identified for process improvement and problem-solving. In *chapter 12* their use will be outlined in detail, both how to use them and when.

Once the culture of the organisation has begun to change and recognition of the needs of the internal customer and supplier have become part of *business as usual*, focus will turn inexorably towards the external customer and supplier. In computer circles the term garbage in means garbage out is well-known. It equally applies to everything we do, especially the processes on which the success of an organisation is based. *Chapter 13* considers how you can influence your suppliers, forming partnerships with them to improve the quality of their inputs to you. Simple methodology for supplier assessment, building regular assessments, by a cross-section of the workforce, into your systems are demonstrated.

You may consider getting an external body to appraise how well you are maintaining quality ideals perhaps using ISO 9000 or the national standard Investors In People. ISO 9000, or BS 5750 as it has previously been known in this country, has had a bad press in recent years. In *chapter 14* we consider the benefits and drawbacks of seeking registration to standards and how to integrate continuous improvement and review into your *business philosophy*.

Finally, the question of keeping up to the mark and ahead of the competition will be considered. *Chapter 15* looks at the task of *benchmarking* individual processes, as well as overall performance. Some consider benchmarking to be an essential element in their quest for continued success; others believe it to be just another management fad. The benefits of benchmarking in a planned manner and building it into the operating systems of the organisation together with a simple model for carrying it out are reviewed.

As with all the material in this book, *you* will make up your mind whether or not it is for you. We hope you will use all of the material which follows and enjoy continued success in the future, having created a *world class organisation* of your own.

1

The Journey through TQM and Beyond

*Building a world class vision for your organisation
as a target for the future*

- Defining the elements that make up total quality management as a foundation for the development of a world class organisation
- Taking a step of faith to change the organisation for ever
- Developing a vision of your organisation as a world class operation
- The world class organisation model

DEFINITIONS

During the 1980s many successful organisations took the advice of the American quality pioneer Dr W Edwards Deming and sought ways of continuously improving their businesses to keep pace with the changing expectations and needs of their customers.

Dr Deming said that a true measure of success in business is demonstrated by the number of repeat customers beating a return path to the door of the organisation. He suggested that simply meeting customers' requirements does not guarantee that they will return again. They may take their custom elsewhere on the basis that they might do better or at least as well. He said they should not simply be satisfied, getting what they want, how they want it; when they want it; they must also be delighted and sent away talking about the organisation if they are ever to return.

He went onto suggest that, if asked, customers probably would not know what their needs and expectations would be if they were eventually to return and that if an organisation waited until then to find out, then it could not expect to be in a position to necessarily meet their new requirements, let alone delight them again. Thus organisations must find ways of continuously improving what they do and the way in which they do it in order to be in the right situation to delight customers again. Unfortunately, the expectations and requirements of our customers, both internal as well as external, are for ever changing and those changes are themselves creating pressure for us to change.

Just for a moment, let us consider what changes have taken place in say the past few years.

During the 1980s we heard a lot about the need to improve personal service and material service. We heard a lot about customer care and improving customer contact skills. We all expect to be treated in a better way. Those expectations are born out of personal experiences of something better and those experiences as customers translate themselves into our experience as employees.

Employees expect to be handled better and expect a higher level of care; we need to improve our *human resource management*, the way we use our people. We can no longer afford the luxury of additional hands. Legislation has changed job security, given more to the part-time worker and provided additional maternity benefits. In Denmark, the father is entitled to the same maternity leave as the mother.

And what about the changes in technology? Computerisation, microchips, point of sale machines, credit cards and Switch. Consider servicing – no longer does the television repair technician carry valves and resistors around, it's all modular; slide something in, take something out. New materials are used and information technology speeds up communications with mobile phones and mobile faxes. This improved technology also leads us to expect better product quality and higher specifications. Every time someone brings out a new advanced whatever, then everyone else must catch up and people expect more and more.

Also, there have been many changes in legislation. New laws have created pressure for change, covering consumer protection liability, health and safety, employment, data protection. All of this forces us to address how we can improve our businesses.

Every change that has even a peripheral effect on our business creates a pressure point for change, as shown in Fig. 1.1. Unless we respond by developing new systems and new methods we will lose out to those who are prepared to change.

So the question must be, what change can ensure continued growth and future strategic success? Your answer must lie in total quality management and world class performance. Through them future business growth and strategic success can't be guaranteed, but can be made a lot more likely.

Those who have chosen to adopt this approach in a structured and systematic way, involving their employees wherever possible and providing a strong and visible lead, by example, from the very top, have begun to reap the benefits in the 1990s. They have also provided models by which we can learn the effective elements of successful programmes of change directed

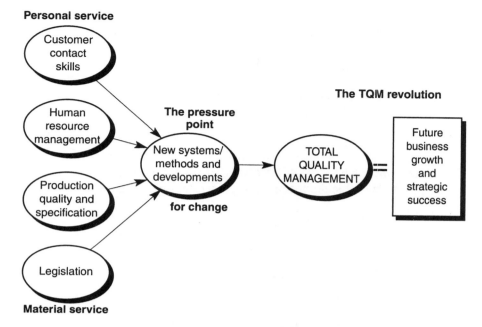

Personal service

Material service

The TQM revolution

Fig 1.1 Pressures to change from change: the evolution of TQM

towards developing what we know as a total quality management culture. One thing the successful programmes have in common is the level of activity and personal involvement by everyone from the top to the bottom of the organisation and across the functions at all levels.

As we entered the 1990s, like so many things, the term total quality management did not quite fit the objective we had and 'world class' became a new term to be applied, describing a successful organisation that attracts more than its fair share of potential customers and employees, is innovative, has an apparently reproducable formula, is just different and better than the others.

Achieving world class performance is a very active thing, it is a state which evolves within an organisation through the active development of a customer focused environment of *free* and *open* communication, up, down and throughout the organisation, of *teamwork* between employees who naturally work together, between employees from different functions and between employees at all levels, and a never ending, *total commitment* to continuous improvement of all they do.

The world's major religions all try to describe a state of grace, being as one with their particular god, a vision of perfection and something that can only be attained by being active and working hard towards it. To a large degree, attaining world class performance or total quality if you wish, has a lot in common with these sentiments. It is a vision of 'perfection' which is unique and personal to each and every organisation. It is something we will only attain by being active and working extremely hard to achieve, with a degree of missionary zeal. And, like the *state of grace*, is something never quite made. However, for the organisation trying to achieve world class performance, it is because the expectations of our *customers* both internal and external are ever changing, forcing our vision to change.

We talk glibly about total quality management and world class performance but what is it?

I have never been happy with any of the definitions provided by the many academics who have written on the subject, so I have attempted to develop a more usable definition, firstly for total quality management:

Total quality management ensures the maximum effectiveness and efficiency of everything that is done within an organisation. It provides market and sector leadership, by the establishment of processes and systems which promote excellence; prevent errors and waste without duplication, and ensures that every aspect of the organisation is aligned to the needs of both the external and the internal customer.

Many people would argue that if their organisation achieved that state or got close to it they would be world class. This is not the case, world class is that and more.

Being world class requires the embracement of the requirements of total quality management as a core, it also requires the development of a *business philosophy* or *formula* that is *unique*, makes the organisation different to others and keeps it different and ahead of others. This unique formula sets the organisation apart from its competitors, creating envy in them, establishes standards of performance, values and behaviour for all, from the most senior to the most humble, and measures, reviews and recognises their achievement.

A world class organisation does not have to operate worldwide, or even nationwide, it may be a small local organisation but one which leads in its area and field, and which embraces and actively demonstrates the characteristics of *world class performance*.

So, a definition of world class performance is:

World class performance maintains continued success through the development of an organisational environment that is distinctly different to peer and competitor organisations in its business philosophy and wealth creating formula. This has been consistently implemented throughout the organisation; embraces and actively maintains a total quality management culture; establishes and continuously develops improved standards of performance which exceed the expectations of its customers, suppliers and employees alike through the devel-

opment and empowerment of its people and the continuous measurement of the needs and satisfaction of its customers, suppliers and its employees.

Examples of this distinctly different *business philosophy* can be found in companies such as Mars, Toyota, Rank Xerox, Motorola, Microsoft, RTZ and Kimberley Clarke. All of these organisations have their own distinctive formula for wealth creation and operational strategy – *the way they do things in their organisation.*

Each maintains continued success through the consistency of the application of its own formula, its simplicity and international transferability, i.e. truly world class.

This has introduced a new phase, business philisophy or operational strategy. I prefer to think of it simply as – *the way we do things around here.*

Many organisations these days declare that they have a *mission statement*, a statement of where they want to be, a *vision* of how and where they see their organisation going in the next five to ten years. Most do not make it because despite having a clear vision of where they want to be, they do not have a clear and stated view of how they are going to get there – a business philosophy.

Let me try to give you a working definition of a business philosophy:

Business philosophy is an explicit expression (usually written down) of the way in which the organisation will achieve its mission; the route map and mode of transport if you like. It details the key activities of the operation and describes the way in which they will be performed in order to be consistently better than anyone else. As well as details of the key activities, all of which must be performed especially well, attention is given to details of the core skills in which excellence is necessary for success.

One of the most common words used in the definitions above is the word customer, internal and external customers, so let us consider what a customer is:

A customer is any individual or organisation who makes a quality judgement about, or has expectations of your output.

The 'your output' part makes it a very personal matter, because we all have customers, both external and internal, and suppliers. One of the foundations of achieving world class performance is having a very clear idea of who your customers are ... what your customers' requirements really are ... how you can delight them ... how you can communicate with them, and know if their requirements change ... how you can maintain continuous improvement of all that you do for them.

This can be equally said of *suppliers.*

REPUTATIONS

In my experience, all organisations compete or are measured by three things, *quality, service delivery* and *price*. What stops them from being world class in terms of quality is the real cost to the organisation of competing on the latter two. If a competitor finds a way of making something cheaper or a competitor for funds can lower their requirements, you will soon find a way of becoming competitive again. The advantage is short-lived.

The same goes for *service delivery*, and here we are not talking just of getting things to the customer on time, we are talking about the whole range of services provided, technology, marketing support, accounts (invoicing arrangements and payment terms), if you find a way of offering more, faster, more reliably, more often, over a wider range, using newer technology than your competitors, i.e. you have a delivery advantage, your competitors will soon find ways of getting back on terms with you.

However, the organisation which steals an advantage on quality, builds a reputation and all that quality implies, it is a gap which the competition finds hard to close.

Reputations for providing a better quality product or service are hard to develop; they take a long time and are therefore long lived and more difficult to counter other than through a long programme of development.

Quality then is the true competitive advantage, a world class foundation.

MANAGING QUALITY

Organisations which took notice of Dr Deming in the 1980s have learned that it is the management of quality which has been the hardest lesson to learn. To become world class, the management of quality is one of the core skills that must be performed consistently well. Some who have made great strides towards achieving what we would term world class performance suggest changing the name total quality management to total *management* quality.

That being the case, perhaps we should attempt to define what we mean by *quality*, then we may have a chance of managing it successfully.

There are many definitions of quality:

- excellence, reliability, goodness (Oxford English Dictionary);
- the totality of features and characteristics of a product or service that bear on its ability to satisfy stated or implied needs (BSI);
- fitness for purpose or function (Joseph Juran);
- Quality = excellence. Excellent organisations do not believe in excellence, only in constant improvement and constant change (Tom Peters).

All are acceptable in their own way, but there is one definition which encompasses all of these without the danger of creating pictures of Rolls Royces, and that is:

Quality is meeting customers' requirements right first time, on time, every time and delighting them in the process by doing that little bit extra that they do not imagine possible.

LEAP OF FAITH OR RATIONAL MANAGEMENT DECISION?

Armed with a definition *quality*, and the certain knowledge of the identity and requirements of your customers and suppliers, both internal and external, you can start to develop a strategic plan to introduce total quality management and world class performance to an organisation. Some would say that to decide to change the whole culture of the organisation requires a large step of faith. However, others who have been able to consider more carefully the true cost of putting things right, internally in order to delivery quality outside the organisation, those who have evaluated the waste in terms of materials and effort and have analysed the effectiveness of some of the key business processes, will say it is the only rational decision that can be made.

Whichever motivates your decision to make a start, if the move to change the organisational culture is to be successful, a plan for change must be carefully developed starting with a vision for the future and a philosophy for achieving it. A strategic plan for the operation of the organisation must be developed and the plan for implementating the cultural change must be linked to the needs of the operational plan as well as the achievement of the vision.

Today almost every organisation seems to talk about quality. Many profess openly to deliver it, and just about as many fail. The main reason for this failure is first, that they do not understand the true meaning of quality, second, they have no formula to ensure they are consistent in what they do; and third, they do not manage its delivery. They do not have a total quality management approach to their organisation's operation.

Total quality management is a methodology for the management of the whole business to improve its effectiveness, flexibility, and competitiveness. It is total because it involves everyone, in every department, getting organised in every activity, at every level. For an organisation to be truly effective, each of its parts must work smoothly with the others, providing quality for each other by meeting each specified requirement, because every activity and every person affects, and in turn is affected by, the others. It does not just happen, the programmes to introduce and to maintain the changes required have to be managed, and more carefully and more closely than anything before.

As we have already stated, all organisations compete, or are measured, on principally three things: quality, delivery and price. There cannot be many senior executives who remain to be convinced that quality is the most important of these. Moreover, as quality improves, costs fall through a reduction in failure and detection costs (it has never been cheaper to do anything twice over). The absence of 'quality' problems also removes the need for the 'hidden operations' devoted to dealing with failure and waste, and delivery performance benefits from increased correct output and higher productivity.

Total quality management is also a method of removing waste, by involving everybody in improving the way things are done. The techniques of TQM can be applied throughout an organisation so that people from different departments and sections, with different priorities and abilities communicate with and help each other. The methods are equally useful in finance, sales, marketing, design, accounts, research, development, purchasing, personnel, computing, distribution, training, after-sales service, warehousing, planning and production.

Total quality management helps a business to:

- focus clearly on the needs of its markets;
- achieve top quality performance in all areas, not just in product or service quality;
- operate the simple procedures necessary for the achievement of a quality performance;
- critically and continually examine all processes to remove non-productive activities and waste;
- see the improvements required and develop measures of performance;
- understand fully and in detail its competition, and develop an effective competitive strategy;
- develop a team approach to solving problems;
- develop good procedures for communication and acknowledgement of good work;
- review continually the processes to develop the strategy of never ending, continuous improvement.

Today's business environment is such that managers must strive for competitive advantage in order to hold on to market share, let alone increase it. Consumers (both internal and external) now place a higher value on quality than on loyalty to their home-based producers and price is no longer the major determining factor in consumer choice. *Price* has been replaced by *quality*. This is true in industrial, financial, service, hospitality, leisure and many other markets. Consumers have ever-increasing expectations and this presents new challenges for the total quality management.

Top managers must understand that TQM is just a concept, a set of guidelines, a model of what is possible. To be successful within an organisation requires careful planning and moulding to meet the specific needs of that organisation. The planning must be strategic and take account of the longer term needs. In its introduction, the plan for implementation must reflect the operational requirements of each department and be seen to be part of the organisation's activities, not an adjunct to them.

DEVELOPING THE VISION

Before a start can be made on the plan for organisational and cultural change, the most senior managers must develop their *vision* for the future of their organisation.

This *vision* must take account of all the factors that impact on the organisation:

- the requirements of the stake holders:
  - shareholders or financial backers;
  - customers;
  - suppliers;
  - employees;
  - the local community;
- the market place;
- regulatory and legislative changes;
- where the organisation is *now* in terms of:
  - market share;
  - product or service life cycle;
  - product or service quality;
  - organisational structure and culture.

Creating a *vision* is not just a cerebral exercise, it is a very practical exercise in visualisation. The senior management group should, in the first instance, brainstorm these impacts and discuss them briefly. In doing so they should try to form a concensus view about the organisation on two levels. Firstly, how does the group see the organisation *now*, i.e. today; secondly the *vision* part, how the group wishes to see the organisation in the future.

These views and ideas must then be documented in the form of two pictures: one – the organisation today; the second – a visualisation of the collective *vision* for the future (how you picture the organisation in, say, five years' time). In producing the two pictures, try to choose a theme which you use for both pictures.

This form of real visualisation of your *vision* of how you wish the organisation to be in, say, five years' time has proved to be tremendous help in developing a clear plan and direction for many organisations, both large and small. Some senior managers find the exercise a little silly, but it is carried out behind closed doors and you are doing it together. My experience of carrying out the exercise with many groups of senior executives, in a wide range of organisations spanning very different cultures, has always been that it is of very positive benefit.

MAKING THE VISION A REALITY

Turning this vision of becoming a world class organisation into reality requires careful implementation planning on two fronts.

1 *Systems and processes* Improving the performance of the organisation's key processes through the identification of those which most affect the achievement of the organisation's business plan; establishing firm improvement targets and milestones to be met within a set time frame; and assigning senior managers to set up and manage teams to bring about the required improvements.

2 *Organisational culture* Creating an environment in which continuous improvement providing measurable results is encouraged. This is done by establishing critical enabling behavioural and cultural mechanisms within the organisation.

This is summarised in Figure 1.2.

If world class performance through total quality management is to be truly effective and the programme of implementation is to create lasting change in the company as a whole then it must be seen to come from the most senior directors starting with the chief executive. All of the senior management team must *visibly* demonstrate their commitment to the programme of change by changing their own behaviour.

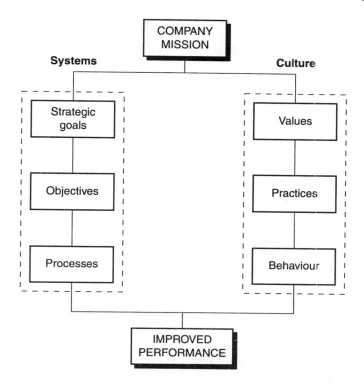

Fig 1.2 Twin-track approach to turning a mission into world class performance

A clear statement of policy towards quality must be established which integrates the implementation programme into the overall strategic plans for the organisation and makes quality and the process of continuous improvement an integral part of those plans.

Middle managers also have a key role to perform. First, they must grasp the principles of world class performance through total management quality and demonstrate their commitment. Second, they must explain the principles to the people for whom they are responsible, ensuring that their own commitment is communicated at the same time. Senior managers must create the environment where the efforts and achievements of their subordinates receive the recognition, attention and reward they deserve. It cannot be stated too often that to be successful in the implementation and maintenance of world class performance, everyone must be involved.

Management's commitment must be obsessional, again starting with the chief executive, who must accept responsibility for quality policy and the strategic plans for its implementation. It is the impact of this person's behaviour, commitment and drive towards changing the culture of the organisation to that of total quality which will have more effect than the most energetic quality manager.

Organisations where a total quality culture and being world class are seen as this year's poster campaign, and are not backed by real commitment from the top, contrast poorly with those organisations where these goals are a reality and can be seen, heard and felt. Systems and techniques are important, but they are not the primary requirement, it is an attitude of mind, a culture based on pride in the job, and requiring *total commitment* from the management which must then be extended to all employees. If the owners and the directors of the organisation do not recognise and accept their responsibilities for the initiation and the operation of each phase of TQM, then the necessary changes will not happen.

Like all changes to organisations, there will be an initial investment requirement, mainly in training and the development of new systems, but like all investments there must be a budget and it must be managed to ensure the right level of return is achieved. The establishment of quality cost models and other benchmarks should be a priority in order to measure progress from an early point.

World class performance is about establishing a commitment to an ideal which embraces the identification of internal and external customers, identifying their requirements and not only meeting them but delighting them; creating an environment where people feel free to communicate when things are right and when they are not; where the culture is to take ownership of one's own quality and measure one's own performance in order to continuously improve it, and where individuals can align their values with those of the organisation and want to be committed.

To assist you to carry out an audit of these factors, Appendix I provides a comprehensive organisational *health check*.

To help you visualise this I have developed a model for world class performance, but I must stress that it is just a model which you may accept or leave as you choose. It does contain the minimum requirements in terms of the foundation stones of achieving world class. Eventually you need to have in your mind your own 'model' of world class. However, in the meanwhile, I urge you to, in the words of the Round Table Movement's motto, 'adopt, adapt, improve'. Adopt it now as a guide, adapt it to suit your needs and those of your organisation and sector, and where you can improve on it, I do not have a monopoly on a vision for a world class organisation.

The model

At the centre of the model is the concept of the internal and external customer and supplier, individually and in the chains that make up the critical organisational processes. World class organisations must be customer-focused in all they do, so this is the foundation of the model (Figure 1.3).

The foundation stone of any 'total quality' or 'world class' culture is the clear understanding and practice, by everyone within the organisation, of the concept of the internal customer–supplier chain. Each of us in any organisation has customers and suppliers, people (individuals) who make judgements or have expectations about the quality of what we do, and about whom we make the same judgements. It must be understood we all have triple roles as customers, suppliers and processors. We take from our suppliers and add value by carring out some process before handling on to our customers. Around this focus on the customer (C) and the supplier (S) linked by a process (p) are the three management elements of the *systems* side of the two-pronged approach to turning the vision into reality and the key management element from the *culture* side (from Figure 1.2). They are:

- process management systems;
- goal driven measurement;

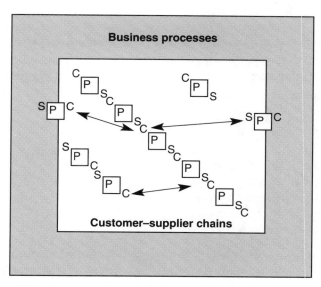

Fig. 1.3 Foundation for a world class model

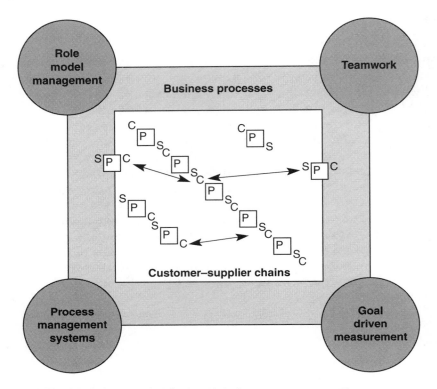

Fig 1.4 World class organisation model: the customer–supplier core

- continuous improvement through the management of people in teams;
- role model management.

Hence, the model develops to form Figure 1.4.

The model core of Figure 1.4 is the active part management has to play in the development of a world class organisation, it is the 'top down' visible commitment to achieving and maintaining the vision. Part of this visibility requires regular review and continuous improvement of the core. The cultural change we have established comes from creating the right environment in which the changes can take place naturally. The elements of this environment are:

- clear leadership and direction from a well-developed mission;
- establishing effective communication up, down and cross the organisation;
- training everyone to identify their customers and suppliers and to recognise the need to meet their requirements every time;

- developing values, practices and behaviours to which all employees can align their own values and help each other to achieve, supported by;
    - an effective system of project management to co-ordinate and manage continuous improvement activity;
    - job enrichment, involvement, good delegation and an air of empowerment felt throughout the organisation;
    - regular appraisal of performance against individual goals and objectives for every one;
    - timely and organisation-wide recognition of success for everybody.

These elements are developed into an environmental model in Figure 1.5.

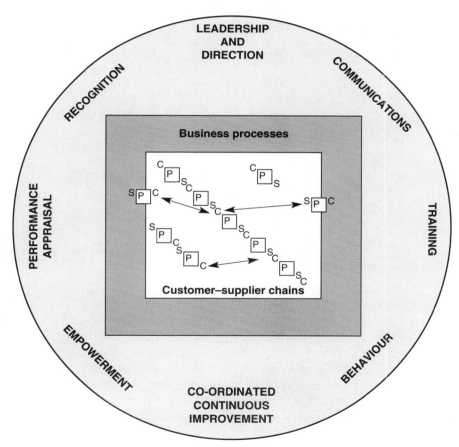

Fig 1.5 World class organisation model: core and environment

Let us consider this model in its entirety (Figure 1.6).

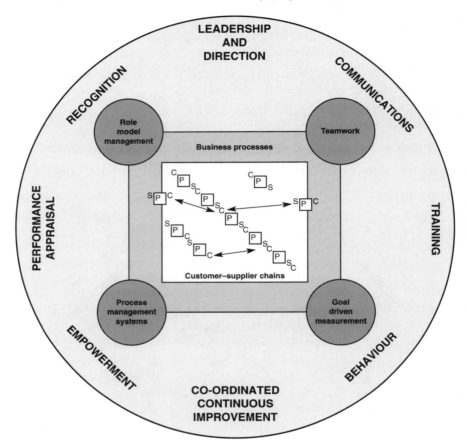

Fig 1.6 Complete world class organisation model

Regular review and improvement of each of these environmental elements, together with regular visits to the mission, the core objectives and the key improvements required to meet future organisational needs, maintains the upward spiral of improvement that helps you to achieve world class performance and drives you forward, keeping you ahead of the competition.

Now, *where are you* on your journey to creating a world class organisation? Using the check list provided as Figure 1.8, consider how your organisation matches up to the model of a world class organisation. Rate your organisation against the criteria scale (Figure 1.9) by describing exactly what you have done.

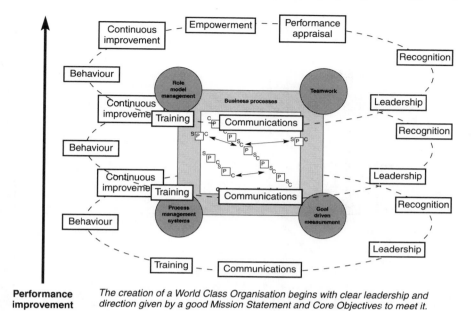

Performance improvement

The creation of a World Class Organisation begins with clear leadership and direction given by a good Mission Statement and Core Objectives to meet it.

Fig 1.7 World class organisation model: continuously improving performance

Put the rating in the square provided. If your rating is 4 or 5, consider how successful the action or policy is today, from the point of view of the 'internal customer' of the policy or system, i.e. your staff, by drawing the faces and expressions as shown.

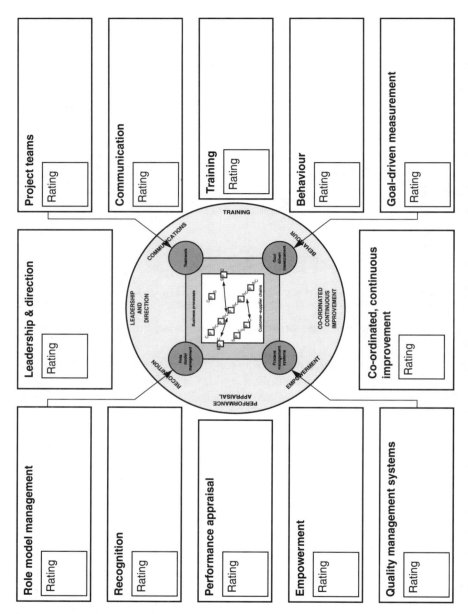

Fig 1.8 Check list: how does your organisation measure up to the model of being world class?

Scale 0 to 5	Rating criteria
0	Never considered doing anything like this
1	Considered doing this, but discarded it as 'not our scene'
2	Tried it once and returned to more traditional methods
3	Had a system like this once, could revive it
4	Have a system for this requirement, but will need rethinking
5	Have systems in place that match this requirement

Performance 0 to 5   **Performance emotion**

0 Does not meet our requirements; might as well not bother

1 If only they would try it, it might work

2 Might be effective if only people were consistent

3 Effective in patches

4 Helps in most cases

5 Meets everyone's requirements and even makes us, the customers, feel good

Fig 1.9 Rate your organisation against the checklist in Figure 1.8

2

Planning for Long-Term Success

Avoiding disappointment by developing a robust implementation plan which includes consideration of all the elements of the world class model.

- The elements of a robust implementation plan
- Combining evolution with the revolution approach
- Focusing on a clear mission and well defined goals
- Linking improvements and necessary changes to a business strategy
- Introducing non-financial performance measurement to monitor process improvements
- Developing a case for change that others will follow

INTRODUCTION

The business world is littered with failed attempts to change the culture of an organisation and to introduce total quality management. The failure can usually be traced to the lack of a clear strategic plan, owned and backed by the most senior managers and which contained actions directly relevant to the needs of the organisation.

TWO APPROACHES TO CULTURAL CHANGE

There are generally two schools of thought with regard to how cultural change and the introduction of practice of continuous improvement should be undertaken: by revolution or evolution.

Revolution

On one side, there are those who believe in revolution rather than evolution. They will tell you that successful change can only be achieved by total and immediate change, swopping 'business as usual' for 'total quality management' overnight. There are many problems associated with this approach, not least of which is understanding the new demands put on organisation by the changes and the expectations that are built up during the implementation phase which middle and junior managers are not able to meet. Managing within the process-oriented structure demanded by total quality management rather than the traditional functionally-oriented one presents it own set of problems requiring careful and measured reactions. Ultimately, this approach fails through the lack of a robust plan which takes into account the potential for the need to fall back on the old 'business as usual' from time to time when the going gets tough during the implementation phase and immediately afterwards.

Evolution

The other school favouring evolution has an implementation plan stretching out over two or three years, learning how to cope with the changing culture a small step at a time, creating islands of excellence and total quality management within the organisation and allowing them to spread out across the organisation organically. This approach can be successful and when it is there is a good foundation of understanding developed in the early stages. The structural changes associated with the move from a functional focus to one based on the customer and the process occurs through a slow evolution. The dangers to this approach occur when 'business as usual' and the 'needs of the business' are cited too often as the reasons for not operating in a total quality fashion. This leads to an erosion of credibility in the plan for change, it takes on a flavour of the month look and eventually leads to the plan being discarded and replaced with something else.

COMBINE THE TWO

The most successful plans for implementing cultural and organisational change take a route somewhere in the middle of these two schools. They are based on four key elements:

1 *A clear mission statement* for the organisation together with identifiable goals, or core objectives, which are individually necessary and together will be sufficient to achieve the mission. Key improvement goals and measures are established, linked to the mission statement and to the core objectives.

A factual case for the need to change the culture and structure of the organisation is developed within this overall plan to support these goals and to assist the understanding of the actions for change.

2 *Management actions* in four key areas: the management of key business processes; the cascade of goal driven measurement; the management of the improvement projects; and the development and visible demonstration of the changes in behaviour through role model management.

3 *An action plan* for the cascade of awareness and training for everyone in the organisation, coupled with a plan of co-ordinated action to establish customer focus behaviour and improvement goals, targets and action at all levels.

4 *Development of the right environment* through a plan to develop and implement the critical environmental factors of communication; training and development; quality values, behaviours and practices; co-ordinated continuous improvement; empowerment; performance appraisal, and recognition.

To these four elements is added a timing plan to complete the overall programme for implementation, as shown in Figure 2.1.

DEVELOPING THE PLAN

Let us look at these four elements more closely.

Clear mission statement

This is the best mechanism for achieving one of the most important responsibilities for the senior managers of any organisation, to provide clear leadership, purpose and direction; which you will recall is the first of the environment changing mechanisms in the model for world class performance developed in chapter 1. The starting point for providing 'leadership and direction' is to have a clear mission statement, owned by all of the senior managers, widely published and explained to all employees.

For those organisations starting out on the implementation of world class performance that do not have a mission statement, one must be developed. For those which do have a mission statement, preparation for the development of an implementation plan provides an opportunity to reconsider:

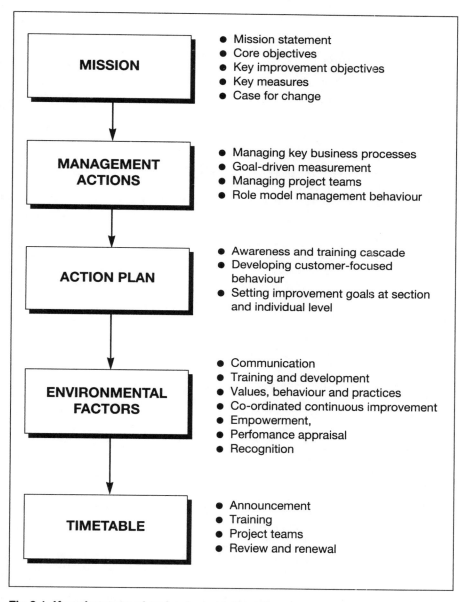

Fig 2.1 Key elements of an implementation plan

- How does it fit with the priorities for a world class organisation?
- Does it need changing in any way?
- How well has it been communicated and understood?

When setting out for the first time to establish a mission statement, it is important to find out what the various stakeholders in the organisation expect of it. They are, the shareholders (if any), the employees, the external customers, the external suppliers and the community in which the organisation is located. It is vital to understand the needs and the expectations of these people prior to constructing the mission. Your mission statement should contain:

- A definition of the business you are in (if this mission is at department of function level the role or contribution of the unit). The worthwhile need(s) to be met and fufilled both externally and internally. Many organisations fail to recognise the crucial importance of adequately defining and then expressing the company's purpose in their mission statements.
- Your distinctive competence, the unique difference between you and the competition.
- Indications of future direction: a brief statement of the main factors to which you would give serious consideration, such as new products or services, new market segments, future development of personnel, etc. These should account for all of your stakeholders' requirements.
- Your principal long-term objective (your ultimate goal) including financial performance if it is appropriate. Making a profit is not a dirty word, and although many organisations shy away from including it in their mission statement, external customers are known to admire suppliers who are bold enough to include financial objectives publicly.

In developing your mission statement you must consider carefully four key points:

- How you intend to satisfy your customers, both external and internal.
- How you intend to release the latent power from within your people and meet their aspirations.
- The level of financial performance required and how you will achieve it.
- How you will introduce a culture of continuous improvement and maintain commitment to it always.

When completed, the mission statement must be documented and agreed by all. Each member of the senior management team must own the organisation's mission statement. If they do not, the process is flawed from conception. It is not enough that it be the chief executive's mission statement; it must be owned by the whole management team. Typically a mission statement can be written down in no more than four sentences and it must be sufficiently explicit to enable eventual accomplishment to be verified. The mission should be subjected to a short test.

First, is it *understandable*? Will the statement be clearly understood by all employees, giving them a common focus and direction for the future? Without a common goal, employees can be like iron filings scattered on a desk top, facing in all directions. If you have a good mission statement that is easily understood, it will act like a magnet being drawn under the table; it will align the filings so that they all point in the same direction, and more than that, they will become magnetised themselves, i.e. it will give them energy.

Next, is it *communicable*? Can it be easily communicated to all stake-holders? Is it easy to explain, first to the staff and then by them to the external customers and suppliers?

Is it *believable*? People must be able to believe that the mission is achievable, maybe not right away, but given the core objectives and the key improvement targets. It does not have to be easy to achieve, but it must be a credible ultimate goal.

Is it *usable*? A mission statement should have two uses. First, as we have already described, as a signpost giving a common direction to everyone. It should be usable in this context to help make decisions, through the simple question: which option will take us closer to achieving the mission? The second use is as a touchstone, helping to define the values, behaviours and practices that will aid eventual achievement and also to return to when the going has been tough for a while and you have been blown off course. It should help you to plot a new course back to the direction of the mission.

Finally, will the *purpose* remain *constant* despite changes in top management? If the mission is the right one for your organisation, the purpose will remain constant for several years even with a change in top management, provided all other factors remain fairly constant.

Strategic goals (core objectives)

As part of your mission statement you must identify the strategic goals or core objectives upon which success in achieving the mission depends. These are the critical factors for success, rather along the lines of the military commander whose mission was to capture a particular town on a high hill. He knew the mission could only be achieved if certain strategic objectives were also achieved.

The critical factors of his success were to take five surrounding hills to provide artillery advantage; clear and secure a main road running between the hills and along the foot of the hill on which the town stood, and to put in place the necessary stocks of supplies and replenishment routes for the final assault. Without each of these strategic goals being achieved *individually* and

Does your mission statement include:

- customer satisfaction?
- people involvement and development?
- financial performance?
- process improvement?
- clear description of the business you are in (your core activities)?
- demonstration of the role or contribution of the unit – for example, profit generator, service supplier, opportunity seeker in terms of needs satisfied or benefits supplied?
- your distinctive competence?
- indications of future direction?

Your mission must be:

- documented;
- agreed by all;
- sufficiently explicit to enable eventual accomplishment to be verified;
- no more than four sentences.

The test is that it should be:

- understandable;
- communicable;
- believable;
- usable.

Some key questions to ask are:

- Does it contain the need that is to be fulfilled?
- Is that need worthwhile (external and internal)?
- Is there a long-term view?
- Does it take into account all the stakeholders in the organisation?
- Will its purpose remain constant despite changes in top management?

Fig 2.2 Mission statement checklist

together, he would not achieve the mission. Each was *necessary* and together they were *sufficient* to complete the mission. In fact, he tried his first assault without having captured the fourth hill. It was almost a disaster, and it was not until he had secured that hill that the mission was finally achievable.

1 Reach £2 billion of profitable annual revenues in telecommunications by the mid-1990s

Be the first choice supplier of the products and services we offer to targeted business and residential markets, through total customer satisfaction.

Be a total quality culture company which fully involves and develops our employees.

2 To provide a total fastenings management service offering logistical solutions for the needs of manufacturing industry.

Our mission is to continuously improve service, systems and product quality to exceed our customers' expectations.

We will achieve this through sustained involvement and development of our people, forming partnerships with both customers and suppliers and the continuous improvement of our processes and facilities, thereby providing superior long-term financial performance.

3 We will be a world class paperboard packaging supplier, exceeding our customers' requirements by investing in the most important resource – our people.

We are committed to:

- creating an environment of participation and involvement for everyone throughout the business;
- a safe workplace;
- continuous training and development of our people;
- the practice of 'doing it right first time';
- proper environment and hygiene practices;
- develop and train self-directed work teams;
- empowerment;
- involving employees, customers and suppliers for continuous improvement;
- pride in performance.

resulting in a customer-focused organisation with low cost, high qualty products and outstanding service.

Fig 2.3 Examples of mission statements

These core objectives are often referred to as the building blocks of eventual achievement of the mission, they are not the 'how to'; the key factors that need to have and which together will deliver the success you seek as an organisation. Often they are not directly manageable, they may contain statements of hope or fear, but they must be supported by clear success criteria. Figure 2.4 gives some examples.

The best place to start defining core objectives is to brainstorm all the possible effects on the eventual achievement of your mission. (If you are unsure of how to carry out a brainstorming activity or whether you are using the best method, turn to chapter 12).

The results of the brainstorm must now be analysed into common areas or themes. An effective method of achieving this is first to consider the common subjects covered by the results and agree a number of headings, then to get each person present to write a number of the brainstorm items onto Post-It notes and to stick these under the appropriate heading on a flip chart or board. (Flip chart paper is excellent for this task because it makes the information visible and can be moved around). Once the possible effects on the achievement of the mission have been categorised in this way, your team can consider the core objectives. Typically, between five and eight core objectives are more than enough. If the mission is simply survival, then four core objectives will be too many. With each core objective, criteria must be set for measuring its eventual accomplishment.

☐ **We must have right first time suppliers**

☐ **We must manage internal relationships**

☐ **We must achieve competitive edge sourcing worldwide from best cost, world class manufacturers**

☐ **We must continuously improve the quality of our service by developing a total quality culture and investing in state of the art systems and technology**

☐ **We must develop products that satisfy current and future market needs**

☐ **We must develop new market opportunities**

☐ **We must achieve a participative management culture**

Fig 2.4 Examples of strategic goals or core objectives

Key improvement objectives

From the mission statement and the core objectives, managers can derive the key process improvement objectives for the business. Then, they can define the key measures for each of those objectives, the appropriate long-term target and the short-term milestones for each measure which are the key drivers in the improvement process. On the face of it, that would appear to be simple and straightforward. Yet it is a process which gives most organisations considerable difficulty. They have difficulty in the sense that they do not identify the core objectives with sufficient clarity and they do not use the objectives and measures decided upon to drive the process forward through the whole company.

At a particular time a company may decide to emphasise or de-emphasise one or two particular core objectives. For example, a business at the forefront of technology may determine that innovation is so vital a part of its business that although properly a subset of customer satisfaction and process improvement, innovation becomes a separately identified core objective.

The resources within any organisation are finite, therefore the resources devoted to process improvement need to be directed towards achieving clear priorities and objectives. What are our priorities for improvement as a company? What milestones do we want to achieve after a year?

Key points for consideration are:

- The senior management team must identify the key processes of the organisation.
- The senior management team clarifies priority areas.
- Have a few, highly visible, company goals with measurements.
- Set specific goals:
    - participatively;
    - avoid general statements;
    - not always easy to do.
- Explain the benefits clearly.
- Improvement objectives should be **SMART** objectives:
  Specific and stretching
  Measured
  Agreed
  Realistic
  Timed.

Identification of key processes for improvement action, which are directly linked to the achievement of the core objectives, gives an extra dimension and impetus to the programme, demonstrating to all the importance of the programme of change within the whole organisation's sphere of operation. To identify the key processes for improvement, you must consider the bigger processes of your organisation, those large customer–supplier chains that are your organisation and are represented at the centre of the model in chapter 1. You will need to use process mapping and analysis (chapter 12) together with results of the development of a cost of quality model (chapter 10).

When you have identified the key business processes, you must determine the degree of impact each has on achieving the core objectives. Simple matrix analysis can help here as shown in Figure 2.5 (also see chapter 12). The objective is to identify those processes which must be carried out particularly well to achieve the core objectives and which offer at this time most opportunity for improvement, i.e. you do not do them very well at this time.

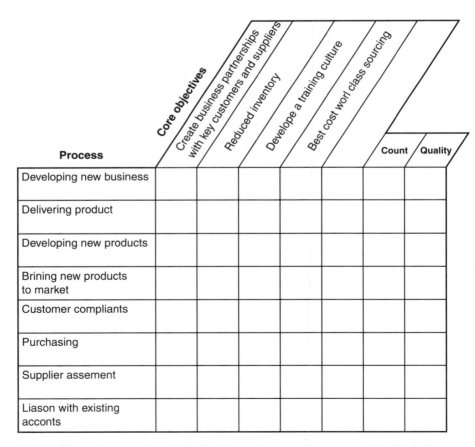

Fig 2.5 Example impact matrix for effect of process on core objectives

For each improvement priority identified, you must develop a proposal that defines the following elements:

- improvement objective statement (including a firm target for the improvement);
- measures to track performance;
- milestones to be achieved during the improvement activity.

An example of an improvement objective statement might be:

'To reduce the waste generated by the development process by 50 per cent of current level by December next year.'

Selection of the improvement priorities should be based on knowledge of the current performance level, customer needs, opportunities for creating a competitive edge and the overall objectives of the business. It is important to look for early success. As part of your preparation you should use the checklist from chapter 1 and carry out a quality cost analysis (described in chapter 10). These results, together with an analysis of the key processes using the process analysis check list from chapter 12, should give you plenty of pointers as to which of the key organisational processes need immediate action and where action needs to be directed.

Key measures

Having identified the core objectives and the key processes which are to be the subject of improvement action, it is necessary to allocate appropriate measures to each. Roger Milliken, the US industrialist said: 'A team without a scoreboard is only practising'. People pay attention to what is measured and tracked; measurement makes accountability clear. The purpose of establishing measures at the outset of the programme is to help ensure that the effect of implementation plans is measured by providing data on progress. This data helps managers adjust the plans as necessary.

Highly visible measurements that indicate progress towards the organisation's process improvement objectives and achievement of the mission are an essential driver of the programme and the performance improvement process. It is not only necessary to have a small number of measurements across the organisation which are tracked by the senior team. It is also necessary to have measurements for each division, department, section and project, to stimulate improvement progress, working with facts rather than opinions as to the effectiveness of the programme and to establish standards.

The effective use of non-financial measurement, as well as financial, to achieve strategic objectives is one of the fundamental messages within the quest for world class performance. Measurement has traditionally been used across organisations as a reporting tool or as a control mechanism, only in some areas has the use of non-financial measurement as a driver for improved performance become established, most commonly in manufacturing. Even in these areas it has developed as a 'bottom up' process with measurement being focused on functional repeated activities. With world class organisation, measurement's role is changed, it becomes as active in the strategic process, a driver of behavioural and process change. For it to play this role, it is necessary that key measures are allocated to each organisational core objective and key improvement objective clearly and unambiguously and communicated throughout the company. *Key measures* must be clear and unambiguous, focused on the organisation's objectives and must be communicated throughout the company.

By definition, those key measures have to be limited in number – no one can manage themselves by a hundred measures – and must be focused upon essential performance elements of the company. The key measures for any activity , department or individual must be limited in number, although below every key measure other measures may exist. Wherever quality improvement is undertaken it is seen to be measured and success thereby recognised. In developing these key measures you should focus only on the organisation-wide measures that the senior team will use to monitor the progress of the implementation process. Typically these measures will:

- be non financial;
- reflect the voice of the process;
- measure non-conformance to requirements, highlight exceptions such as things going wrong;
- concentrate on the critical few, which will be important for the customer.

You should consider the elements which are important for developing and maintaining competitive edge. Think about which vital signs in the process you will measure. Then, ensure they:

- have a link to the mission statement;
- are prominently displayed;
- are consistent, and that you avoid frequent changes.

Finally, as a guide to setting measures, consider the following:

- Measure things that people can see and understand.
- Capture the voice of the customer and the voice of the process.
- Measure the things that are wrong.

- Concentrate on the vital few; too many measures are counter productive, become bureaucratic and wasteful.
- Encourage ownership through self tracking and reporting – trust people.
- Make the data public, within the business unit.
- Wherever possible, use established data and measures.

Measurement by itself cannot bring about improvement and therefore should never be carried out without the data being used with the tools for improvement. Part of ensuring the successful implementation of a programme to develop a world class organisation is to have visible signs of the continuous improvement process (plan, do, check, act, see chapter 9) being used every day, not just for improvement projects. As part of the proposals for measurement, plans are required to encourage the daily use of the PDCA cycle and the improvement tools.

Consideration should be given to building some of the simple tools into everyday operations and then the planned introduction of the more sophisticated tools. A training need should be recognised and catered for in the proposals, not for everyone but for a number of enthusiastic managers and others who show an interest to undertake specialist training and refresher courses.

Consider the example of '*we must provide customer satisfaction*' as a core objective, the identification of the measures is reasonably clear. What is it that customers requires of a supplier? First, they require delivery of a product or service. That product or service must be delivered complete and in a timely manner. Therefore the company should measure its delivery performance in terms of both completeness and time. The customers require products that are supplied free of defects. Therefore each company should measure its performance in the supply of defect-free product to its customers. Customers also want an error-free relationship with the supplier. Therefore the appropriate measure of the error content in the relationship must be identified, for example by credit notes. In addition to these specific measures of performance, it is necessary to measure customer satisfaction in a more general sense. Therefore regular and frequent customer surveys provide an appropriate measure.

Key measures for the objective '*we need to provide high levels of training and development*' will relate to the effectiveness of communication, the availability and effectiveness of training, appraisal and development opportunities. Again, there will need to be a general measure of people satisfaction through the process of a satisfaction survey.

'*Process improvement*' is a more difficult objective for which to identify appropriate key measures. However, they do exist and are capable of clear expression. Process improvement can be measured by:

- cycle time;
- waste – in a broad sense, of raw materials, utilities, machine down time, under-used capacity, people;
- productivity.

The measurement of '*we must continue to provide current levels of financial performance*' presents a different challenge – that of identifying key measures from the large number of financial measures that exist. Some are obvious, such as return on capital employed, return on sales, percentage contribution and overheads. Some are less obvious and may well be of a different nature in different companies. It is essential that managers identify for their organisation its own the core objectives, improvement goals and measures.

A case for change

You have now completed the important task of providing the leadership and direction required of the implementation process. You have: a mission statement, a set of core objectives (or strategic goals); key improvement objectives relating to the essential organisational processes; and have established measures for both the core objectives and the improvement objectives together with longer term targets and milestones. You know where you are going and how you intend to get there.

To complete this part of the implementation plan, you must now consider the case for the reasons for change which you wish to present to your organisation. You must examine the declared personal actions and behaviours you intend to introduce and be prepared to explain *why*. This will go a long way to providing a solid foundation for the implementation programme and avoid it becoming flavour of the month. Here are some key points to bear in mind.

Commitment is demonstrated by:

- sound business reasoning;
- clear leadership;
- changing personal actions and behaviours;
- sharing and implementing the vision and mission.

Commitment is maintained by:

- review against plan;
- feedback from staff;
- revisiting the mission;

- quarterly critique of actions;
- asking, what signals did we send?

Your commitment will always be challenged.

The overall direction must also be considered from the viewpoint of the employees to whom it is to be communicated:

- Is it communicable?
- Is it believable?
- Does it give a clear lead and direction?
- Is there a clear path to what next?

If the answer to any of these questions is 'no' or even a 'maybe' then further development is required before it is ready for delivery.

Finally, the question is put: 'Are we committed?' There should be no hesitation on the part of any member of the senior management team as to the plans and the reasons for the changes proposed. You will be challenged and any doubts will be found out.This first element of the implementation plan is critical for getting the rest right. In itself, it provides the senior team with leadership and direction and if communicated well will provide a focus, the need for change and direction for all staff.

THE MANAGEMENT ACTIONS

Once the mission, together with the associated goals, objectives, targets and measures, has been completed and agreed, the senior team must turn its attention to the four *management action areas*. These are the active and very visible demonstrations of commitment, by the senior management, which will help to create the environment in which all employees will realise that the efforts to change the culture and focus of the organisation are not just words and exhortations, but are real and achievable. These are the actions that will enable the environmental issues to become part of 'business as usual' and help people to feel truly empowered.

Process management systems

Once the key processes of the organisation have been identified and mapped, methods of managing these processes across the functional boundaries have to be agreed and put in place. Consideration must be given to the structure of the organisation. Is the structure sufficient to allow the proper management of the delivery of quality and the continuous improvement of the key processes of the organisation? What we are trying to achieve is a structure that is focused on the customer in terms of:

- providing total quality according to the definitions we have developed,
- preventing things going wrong rather than finding things have gone wrong after the event;
- allowing for controlled change where it is necessary.

Within each process everyone must know their individual responsibility for the quality of what they do. There need to be mechanisms for feeding back data on the effectiveness of the process and the individual activity; for determining the level of customer satisfaction; and for when customers, change their requirements. In effect, each of the key processes of the organisation is a mini quality management system which will meet the requirements of ISO 9000. A good guide to the requirements of good process management systems can be found in those applications which surround the ISO 9000 standard itself (ISO 9000-1, ISO 9000-2 and ISO 9004).

Regular methods of review of both process capability and process effectiveness need to be included in the system for managing them. This will include a management team formed from those individuals who manage particular parts of the process and local workgroups who can carry out team purpose analysis and departmental purpose analysis to establish customer–supplier agreements between the individual activities that make up the process itself.

Some organisations find when they have reviewed their key processes and are looking for ways of establishing systems to manage them, that an entirely new structure is appropriate for the whole organisation. If this is the case and the mood is right then we have a revolutionary change which must be planned even more carefully. Particular emphasis must be paid to any new skills required by those people who will be asked to manage the change. Further, they will need coaching in how to change the style of management and leadership so that the benefits are maximised.

Development of management systems to meet the ISO 9000 standard for total quality management systems is discussed in more depth in chapter 14.

Goal driven measurement

We have discussed the use of organisational goals (core objectives) and improvement goals to establish key measures earlier in this chapter. Managers now need to take this approach into their functional area and if they are responsible for key processes to that level also. Using team purpose analysis or departmental purpose analysis to focus attention on the key role of the department, function or process, a local mission or strategic objective can be established. Core objectives can be established once the mission is agreed and key improvement targets. Local action plans can be drawn up and key measures of performance improvement signed.

Once again, regular reviews must be established to ensure that improvement in performance in taking place and to modify action plans where necessary.

Figure 2.6 demonstrates the process of cascading goals and goal-driven measurement into the body of the organisation right down to the level of the individual.

To close the loop on goal-driven measurement, we need to establish a performance appraisal scheme which links the improvement goals of the

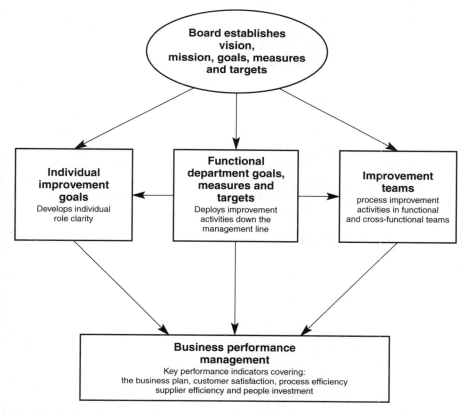

Fig 2.6 Goal and measurement cascade

company, the department, and the individual with some form of recognition. Regular appraisal provides the opportunity to coach individuals to enable improved performance to take place and to identify further opportunities for improvement.

The active establishment by management of process measurement and individual measurement is a key activity in demonstrating the reality of the organisations' main mission and its core objectives. This brings the mission closer to individuals within the organisation and provides daily, visible evidence of their importance.

Managing project teams

The third management action is the management of project teams to achieve the key process improvements identified by the mission and the core objectives. Providing a structure to capture opportunity for improvement ideas and to convert those ideas into actions, either by individuals or through the formation of improvement teams, is not by itself sufficient to create the environment where individuals feel involved in the continuous improvement process and feel empowered to make change. All too often such structures are established but 'the needs of the business' get in the way of prioritising this activity. Effective management of project teams gives continuous improvement the desired level of importance within the organisation. At the same time, it prevents the organisation falling into the 'activity trap' where lots of effort is being put into team meetings to the detriment of normal organisational activities and with the achievement of little progress. Techniques for the effective management of project teams and natural work teams are investigated in some detail in chapter 8.

Role model management

The first three management actions deal principally with the systems side of Figure 1.2 showing the twin track for converting a vision of a world class organisation into the reality of improved performance and increased reputation. The active and visible demonstration of role model management establishes the values, practices and behaviours that are required to achieve the cultural and organisational changes that will create the world class organisation.

Role model managers always act as a role model for their employees: i.e. they exemplify by their behaviour the qualities that they wish their people to display and by their example encourage the adoption of those qualities by others. They are customer-focused, fact-based managers, using measurement in the achievement of their goals, listening to their people, recognising performance, empowering, trusting and coaching.

This issue is dealt with in more detail in chapter 3 together with methods of establishing the key elements of role model management behaviour in your organisation.

THE ACTION PLAN

Other 'enabling' disciplines that must be developed from the company workshop and implemented while creating project teams must take into account a range of policies, as listed in Figure 2.7. The establishment of these enabling mechanisms cannot of itself change the culture of a company. They can facilitate the management of the business. However, managers have to change their behaviour and leadership styles to make the cultural change happen. It is the management's behaviour which makes the essential difference, much more than new facilities or new investment.

In the words of a British employee after working in a Nissan factory in Japan: 'It was not as high-tech as I expected, the machines were largely the same as the British plants. The difference was all about philosophy, management and the use of resources. I was dazzled by how simple the Japanese approach seemed.'

People will not believe you unless your behaviour changes.

- **Communication** Two-way, up, down and across the organisation, involving everyone, in formal and informal communications and a newsletter.

- **Project management** To maximise the involvement of everyone in the improvement process, by cascading the goals and measures to every part of the business and managing the 'bottom up' opportunities for improvement.

- **Recognition** Formal polices to recognise performance.

- **Reporting** Ways must be established of reporting company and group measures, progress on the implementation and the improvement efforts in a formal way to the business and to the quality support team.

- **Performance appraisal and review** A formal system must be developed, based on the newly introduced group system, and implemented.

▶

Fig 2.7 The action plan should take account of these enabling mechanisms

- **True customer focus**

  - Continually monitor the quality of the service we provide to customers.
  - Senior managers should regularly involve themselves at the customer interface to both verify and experience the quality of customer service.
  - Organisations must be customer-friendly through every aspect of their business; ease of telephone communication; the quality of the product; the quality of the catalogue; the timeliness of deliveries.
  - Each business must adequately research customers' requirements and their perception of our performance against their requirements.
  - Customers and their requirements must be at the centre of all meetings and business decisions.

- **Effective internal communications**

  - An organisation must place strong emphasis upon effective internal communications.
  - An organisation must communicate effectively with all of its people.
  - People must be able to communicate easily and effectively with their senior management.
  - Their senior management must listen to that communication.

- **Training and development culture**

  - People are seen as the major asset which makes the organisation unique.
  - That asset and unique resource should be continually developed.
  - The major element in that development is training.

- **Empowered employees**

  - In a **total quality** company, individuals are well trained and well motivated, with good lines of communication, and thus *are* empowered.
  - **Empowerment** carries with it responsibility and accountability and within total quality companies individuals will see empowerment as a recognition of their abilities and be further motivated.

- **Established recognition culture**

  - A total quality company recognises success rather than failure, and most of all recognises performance.

- **Effective and goal-driven measurement**

  - Total quality companies do not simply focus on financial measurement. They also focus on non-financial performance across a wide spectrum

Fig 2.7 contd.

of business activities. Such non-financial measurement is a vital tool by which the business can be improved.

'Financial reporting is like a school report card, it tells you how you have done as you start the summer holidays'. Non-financial measurement however is an immediate tool. It provides information at the moment of activity of, for example, non-achievement of time and delivery targets, failure to meet sales call targets, etc. More importantly, the drivers and storekeepers know as it happens, the sales people know it, as do their managers. Corrective action can therefore be taken immediately and frequently by the relevant employee without reference to their manager.

- **Clear focus upon process improvement**

  – **Total quality** companies continually look at their processes, looking critically at the sequence of activities that together produce the outputs of their business.
  – A major strategic benefit of continual analysis is the reduction in cycle time of all activities as they optimise the way they work together within the organisation.

- **Continuous Improvement**

  – Total quality companies see that big wins are not enough. They look for every day, every week improvements. The Japanese call it *kaizen*, but it is not Japanese. Thomas Carlyle expressed a similar sentiment in the 1860s. 'It is a mathematical fact that the casting of this pebble from my hand alters the centre of gravity of the universe.'

- **Leadership and direction**

  – Every **total quality** company has a real mission statement which everyone understands and which is available to every one.
  – A spectrum of measurable improvement goals are agreed, including everything from earnings per share, to complete on time deliveries, to a number of days of training per employee.
  – Managers change the way in which they perform their role. They coach, trust and empower their people, and actively move away from traditional managerial behaviours.

Fig 2.7 contd.

3

Leading the Charge

Developing the right management style to provide senior management leadership of the drive for change

- **The level of visible commitment required from senior managers including the chief executive to be truly successful**
- **Understanding what behavioural style the employees will follow**
- **What constitutes role model management and process-oriented behaviour?**

INTRODUCTION

One of the key differences between those cultural change programmes which succeed in introducing a total quality culture and move the organisation towards becoming world class and those which are doomed to failure from inception is the adoption by senior managers of a new and visible management style. This demonstrates clearly the values, practices and behaviours required of the changing organisation.

In 1988, British Airways had completed a huge initiative to change the company's image prior to privatisation. A lot of money was spent training all staff to recognise the internal as well as the external customer, to understand their requirements and to have a more acute awareness of the interdependence of each function. BA commissioned research to determine if all the investment had improved its image with passengers. To the amazement of the directors, the initial reports suggested that the passengers were neutral, just that the image was no worse. However, the interesting information came in supplementary reports which indicated clearly that the employees were watching the behaviour of the management more closely than the passengers were watching the company. The reports went on to demonstrate that visible and active changes in senior management behaviour were absorbed very quickly into the culture of the organisation, almost as unofficial company policy. Thus it can be seen that successful cultural change initiatives directed towards world class performance are led by senior management role models.

We saw in the first chapter, Figure 1.2, that there are twin tracks in the successful carrying forward of the mission into a genuinely improved organisational performance. Developing and supporting process management systems, goal-driven measurement and using people in project teams to improve the key processes of the organisation are all *activities* which support the left hand, 'systems', arm of the model. Role model management behaviour, coupled with role model behaviour between everyone in the organisation, process leaders and team members, is the critical *activity* which supports the right hand, 'culture', arm of the model.

In this chapter we talk about 'role model management' behaviour in general terms. Each organisation will have its own particular *values*, *practices* and *behaviours* which must be identified and followed for this activity to be totally successful. A survey must be conducted within the organisation to tease out these important behavioural factors. Figure 3.1 shows the type of questions which may be included in an employee survey.

ROLE MODEL MANAGEMENT

Role model management is the term given to a style to be adopted by all senior managers and transferred by example to all other members of management and supervision – anybody who has someone reporting to them. To be a role model which will help to establish the right environment for cultural change you must be:

- customer-focused;
- people-focused;
- demonstrate personal integrity;
- visible;
- a promoter of excellent standards;
- a challenger of the status quo.

Be customer-focused

To be focused on the customer means knowing your internal and external customers and finding out and understanding exactly what they require now and in the future. It is demonstrated by regularly using and referring to tools such as 'departmental purpose analysis' and 'team purpose analysis' and 'customer–supplier agreements' both formally and informally. Being customer-focused also means encouraging feedback and reacting to

	Strongly disagree	Disagree	Neutral/ not sure	Agree	Strongly agree
1 We know what our customers do with our products or how customers use our services.	1	2	3	4	5
2 We are good at keeping up with the changing needs of our customers.	1	2	3	4	5
3 We are better at giving customers what they want than our competitors.	1	2	3	4	5
4 We do a better job of delivering our products or services on time than we did a year ago.	1	2	3	4	5
5 We respond better to customers' problems now than we did a year ago.	1	2	3	4	5
6 We do whatever it takes to satisfy a dissatisfied customer.	1	2	3	4	5
7 People inspect their own work rather than rely on others to do it for them.	1	2	3	4	5
8 We are completely clear about what our customers' requirements are.	1	2	3	4	5
9 The company works to improve its ability to measure how well it meets customers' requirements.	1	2	3	4	5
10 I get information about problems with my work in sufficient time to deal with them.	1	2	3	4	5
11 Other people/departments create unnecessary work for me/my department.	1	2	3	4	5
12 The work I receive from other departments has been done correctly.	1	2	3	4	5
13 We treat other departments and people in the company as well as we treat our customers.	1	2	3	4	5
14 My department regularly receives feedback from other departments about how well we meet their requirements.	1	2	3	4	5

Fig 3.1 Outline for employee survey

it with mutually-agreed actions. It means using customer satisfaction as a key measure in all business decisions, and giving excellent service to all your customers, internal and external all of the time.

The 'customer-focused' manager discourages departmentalism and blinkered attitudes, helping the team to understand the broader picture and the way they fit into the company as a whole.

Be people-focused

To be truly people focused means showing fairness, trust, and respect to everybody unless you have very good reasons to do otherwise. Managers should encourage honest feedback and encourage open debate. People-focused managers keep their team well-informed about expectations and performance, ensuring that they receive relevant department, function and company information. They are responsive to questions and requests raised by team members.

Being people-focused requires the giving of the responsibility, the authority and the support to act, to people working for you and making sure that their contributions are recognised. Empowering within clear limits and facilitating with appropriate allocation of coaching and coun- selling resources. It means developing the skills of your people through training and the provision of experience opportunities, work shadowing, meetings, cross-functional teams and the like. Pro-actively looking for opportunities for them to widen their experience.

Setting and agreeing specific, measurable, agreed, realistic and time- bound objectives for your staff, being perceptive to their concerns and carrying out effective performance reviews regularly, both formally and informally, at frequent intervals, once a year is not enough; most individu- als want to know and care about how they are doing. Encouraging personal development is another element, not just those who report directly to you but all those with whom you have contact. Role model man- agers are natural coaches and provide the time to help people develop.

Demonstrate personal integrity

There is only one way to establish the values, behaviour and practices with which you wish the whole organisation to align themselves -- by demon- strating personal integrity in all managers and supervisors. It means doing exactly what you say you will do, when you say it will be done. It means being punctual and well prepared at all times and especially for meetings when other people's time may be wasted if you are not, particularly where subordinates are likely to attend.

Ensuring that you and your people deliver on time, whatever it is. You use and give feedback constructively and openly. You act honestly in all your dealings with people inside and outside of the organisation.

You are open about errors and learn from them.

You do not gossip or actively feed the organisational grapevine. You respect other people's views and confidences and spend time and energy ensuring adherence to agreed values, thereby creating an atmosphere of mutual trust and not reacting in an emotional or aggressive manner to errors and omissions on the part of others.

Make yourself visible

Role model managers are required to be open and accessible, not just publicising an open door policy, but taking the open door to the employees and staff by regular walkabouts, 'walking the talk' to break down the 'us and them' barriers and humanising the process of leadership . Not everyone can leave the job to make use of the 'open door' policy. Words are easy ... 'I am always available ...' You must be actively visible if you want to catch people doing things right and give them recognition that will change the culture from that of the 'cop' who always finds people doing things wrong.

Being visible and 'walking the talk' helps to develop good relationships and informal dialogue with the whole workforce. It is often known as 'management by walking about' (MBWA). By doing so you find out early about quality problems and can clearly communicate commitment to, and support of, the total quality process. Your visibilitys helps to support and encourage teamwork, especially the sense of the wider, complete organisation team. It provides the opportunity to encourage openness and approachability and for managers to stay up to date with developments within the company, especially if you 'walk the talk' in departments and functions other than your own.

Promote excellent standards

Promoting excellent standards gets rid of the general acceptance of failure that is one of the common characteristics of more traditional organisations. To do this you need to set quality measures and targets for your own work, use all available data when evaluating situations and insist that output always meets or exceeds agreed specifications. The role model manager is then seen to be working to prevent errors rather than reacting to them by setting demanding, but SMART targets, as in chapter 2, and making them visible. By holding effective meetings, making quality a key agenda item every time and personally using the processes, tools and techniques of total quality, you encourage others to use them and continue to look for better ways of doing things.

Publicising achievements helps the communication of the right messages and demonstrates to the sceptical ones that change is not only possible but is happening right there and then. Role model managers are always leading by example.

Challenge the status quo

If the culture of continuous improvement is to be nurtured, role model managers must be seen to be forever challenging any work that does not contribute to quality output, openly welcoming new ideas from others and to be listening with an open mind and responding. They will not allow departmentalism or a blinkered attitude to influence decisions, always encouraging the process of seeking opportunities for improvement from what ever source.

Managers should fully support agreed decisions to implement change, and encourage a 'no recrimination' climate. This is augmented by actively seeking challenging opportunities and continually describing the future that you wish to build together.

Role model behaviour is not the sole domain of senior managers. If the initiative to change the culture is to be successful, then role model behaviour must be visibly demonstrated by the whole workforce to one another – managers, supervisors, everyone.

Generally it is an improvement in personal service to each other that is a prerequisite: people treating each other as real customers and according them the same high standard of 'customer care' and service as we expect as external customers in shops, banks, restaurants, etc.

Peer and subordinate review

Role model managers are constantly looking to improve and a tool that they might consider employing is 'peer or subordinate review'. This requires considerable personal courage initially as managers are not conditioned to take feedback from their peers or subordinates on their personal behaviour. Under traditional values it may be seen as a sign of weakness, but in a total quality culture it is seen as a genuine attempt at continuous improvement.

To carry out the review, a checklist or questionnaire is required, providing a list of the criteria you have agreed constitute role model management within your organisation. Figure 3.2 shows a typical check list which you may like to use, if you are feeling particularly courageous. It is probably best used initially between the members of the senior management team. Each individual rates the role model management performance of each of their peers and the recipient collates the results. In an atmosphere of openness and trust, they reveal the overall results to their colleagues and include an action plan for improvement. Each plan is approved as worthy by the whole team.

This is then repeated in the early stages at, say, three-monthly intervals. To demonstrate true commitment to the process, the manager gets their own teams to appraise their performance as a role model manager.

For all who are, or aspire to be, the leaders of cultural change in the development of a world class organisation there are particular standards of behaviour that are expected of you by your people and your colleagues. *You* are expected to be a total quality champion at all times and are expected to:

- Be customer-focused
- Be people-focused
- Demonstrate personal integrity
- Be visible
- Promote excellent standards
- Challenge the status quo

How do you measure up?

Are you customer focused?	Sometimes	Most of the time	Always
1 Do you know who your internal and external customers are?			
2 Do you establish agreements with your customers and suppliers?			
3 Do you arrange 'twinning' visits with other relevant departments?			
4 Do you set and measure targets based on meeting customer requirements?			
5 Do you display products and service information with which work teams are associated?			

Fig 3.2 Checklist for role model leadership

Are you people focused?	Sometimes	Most of the time	Always
6 Do you ensure clear individual and team goals are established?			
7 Do you empower within clear limits and facilitate achievement with appropriate resource allocation?			
8 Do you display individual and team achievements?			
9 Do you schedule regular review of individual objectives and contribution plans?			
10 Do you plan 'spontaneous' recognition?			
Do you demonstrate personal integrity?	Sometimes	Most of the time	Always
11 Do you do what you say you will do?			
12 Are you punctual and well prepared?			
13 Do you deliver requirements on time or even earlier than agreed?			
14 Do you use feedback constructively?			
15 Are you open and honest about errors and learn from them?			
Are you visible?	Sometimes	Most of the time	Always
16 Do you target, schedule and measure the effectiveness of 'walkabout' time?			
17 Do you catch people doing things right and recognise it publicly?			
18 Do you formally evaluate meetings?			
19 Do you encourage openness and approachability?			
20 Do you instigate visible mechanisms to promote and capture ideas?			
Do you promote excellent standards?	Sometimes	Most of the time	Always
21 Do you set quality measures and targets for your *own* work?			
22 Do you insist that outputs meet or exceed agreed specifications?			

Fig 3.2 Contd.

	Sometimes	Most of the time	Always
23 Do you schedule specific and regular team time for improvement activity?			
24 Do you set demanding but SMART targets and make them visible?			
25 Do you personally use the processes, tools and techniques of total quality and encourage others to use them?			
Do you challenge the status quo?	*Sometimes*	*Most of the time*	*Always*
26 Do you openly challenge any work or activity that adds no value to quality outputs?			
27 Do you welcome new ideas from others, listening with an open mind and responding flexibly?			
28 Do you actively seek challenging opportunities for improvement?			
29 Do you actively discourage departmentalism and blinkered attitudes to change?			
30 Do you identify the 'totally' and 'partially blind' and create positive plans to help them to become committed?			
How did you do?	*Sometimes*	*Most of the time*	*Always*
Total scores			
For each score multiply by the following weighting factor	0	2	5
Add these totals			
Total score			
Target			150

If you really feel brave, now get two or three of your colleagues to complete this about *you* and discuss the results with them. Such openness can be extremely useful.

Better get your team to complete the questionnaire about the way they see your behaviour and publish the results after discussing ways of improvement with them. That is *role model management*

Use this checklist every three months to check your progress in developing role model behaviour.

Fig 3.2 Contd.

PROCESS TEAM LEADER BEHAVIOUR

Process team leaders, the middle managers and supervisors, also have an important role to play in the demonstration of the values, practices and behaviours required of a world class organisation. Besides following the same role model behaviour codes as senior management, they must also take care to give the right signals throughout the daily routines. They must always focus on the element of *delighting the customer,* not just meeting their requirements, and seeing and treating everyone in the process as a *customer* irrespective of the functional boundaries. Supervisors need to see the whole organisation as a customer–supplier network, knowing their own customers and suppliers and developing open, trusting, win–win relationships with them. A commitment to using *customer–supplier agreements* (see chapter 12), both formal and informal, is crucial to establishing relationships based on interdependency rather than hierachy. Such agreements can also help treat external suppliers as part of the process.

Team leaders see themselves as responsible for their own activities. They map processes and take active steps to gain and maintain control of them. As managers they must be prepared to say *no* if it will enable others to do *quality* work. The process leader is the true driving force for continuous improvement, allocating resources to improving the process, breaking down the functional barriers and resolving functional conflicts. They will empower team members to continuously identify and implement improvements, driving and stimulating the continuous improvement process itself by using total quality tools where appropriate, working with facts not opinions, solving problems not symptoms, always aiming for simplicity, having process measurements in place and encouraging everyone to measure their own performance.

In establishing agreements between customers and suppliers, they will set goals and objectives and put process measurements in place that will delight the customer with knowledge of process capability. Behaviourally, they will lead with a participative style, promoting teamwork, developing job descriptions which are focussed on the customer and process. They will give visible recognition in acknowledgement of contributions from other.

TEAM MEMBERS

Finally, let us examine the role all employees can play in developing the desired cultural environment through their own behaviour. To start creating the right conditions to change the attitudes within your organisation everyone must provide a high level of *internal customer care*. This can be achieved by following the rules of delivering good customer service used by the retail industry:

- *Rule 1*   The *customer's* requirements are our business. That is what we are there for.
- *Rule 2*   *Customer's* are not interested in our problems. They are only interested in theirs.
- *Rule 3*   You can only tell a *customer* something when you have earned the right to do so by listening to them first.

These three simple rules must be supported by behaviour in employing the ten basic steps in delivering good *Personal Service*:

- smile;
- give eye contact;
- use people's names;
- give people your full attention;
- match body language and create rapport;
- match speech in terms of using the same vocabulary again to create rapport;
- show respect for other points of view;
- support your colleagues (do not let them down to others);
- always have pride in your job however apparently lowly (every job is important);
- dress the part.

In addition to providing good personal service to each other, as between supplier and customer, team members must behave as they would wish others to behave, providing role models for fellow employees to follow by themselves being:

- *Customer focused*

    - Identify customers and suppliers.
    - Communicate regularly with customers to ensure customers needs are known and suppliers know theirs.
    - Listen to them and respond.

- *Process-oriented*

    - Team members take responsibility for their part of the process.
    - Understand the whole process.
    - Identify opportunities for improvement.
    - Actively participate in implementing process improvements.

- *A team player*

  - Recognise that team strength is greater than the sum of the individual efforts.
  - Promote participation in teams.
  - Encourage consensus reaching in setting goals and solving problems.
  - Use the team environment to learn and grow.
  - Keeps the team well informed and shares knowledge.

- *A TQ champion*

  - Actively champion the TQ approach.
  - Promote the continuous improvement culture.
  - Measure and monitor themselves.
  - Promote people development.
  - Identify sceptics and help them to convert.

Determining customers' requirements is traditionally the role of the sales or marketing department. Certainly with a total quality management approach, everyone is called upon to qualify their internal customers' requirements and to record any changes as they arise. This will demand some internal marketing and training of individuals to be aware of their changed role, in order to set up this informal marketing department.

Externally, the marketing people will have an increasingly important role in determining and forecasting future requirements in order to plan the direction of continuous improvement to meet future strategic needs.

4

Preparing Managers and Supervisors

*It will be too late if you wait for change to happen before you
prepare your managers and supervisors to handle the change*

- Reasons for investing in your people
- How to unlock leadership potential
- Skills required to manage change
- Communication skills checklist
- Human relationships and teamwork checklist
- Effective meetings skills checklist
- Problem-solving and decision-making checklist
- Power user's checklist
- Motivating people to follow you
- Staff motivation checklist

INTRODUCTION

Developing *role model behaviours* will not be enough in itself to ensure a smooth transition from a traditional culture to a total quality culture. It is an unfortunate fact that as soon as the change starts to take place there is real risk of senior and middle managers themselves becoming the blocks and barriers to change and progress. Unless they have been prepared properly and completely before hand they will not know how to cope with or respond to the results and the effects of the changes. The same to a lesser, but nonetheless real, extent is true of other employees who will lack skills to meet the new challenges of empowerment, leading teams, investigating problems and so face a barrier to their progress and total commitment.

The introduction of total quality management and progression towards becoming a world class organisation is based on releasing the latent power within your people. It was Tom Peters who said '... people don't hang their brains up with their coats in the morning when they arrive at work.' Traditional management treats its staff as if they do, whereas an inventory of employees' outside interests, most often demonstrates a wide range of skills and positions. These skills are found within organisations in senior management teams, but within the workforce in general in their outside activities. Peter Janzen, chief executive of Caradon plc, maintains that the only real difference between organisations is their people and it is the ability to unlock their potential that is the difference between good companies and world class companies.

To unlock this potential you need to approach it on two levels. First will be personal development for managers to prepare them for the changes that are going to take place and their changing role. Added to this will be a recognition that new core skills will be required and so training must be planned.

Second will be development of the rest of the workforce so they can play a full part in the changes and to take on the responsibilities that will come with empowerment. In this area you need to address the awareness of the total quality implementation process and the overall plan and awareness of other people's jobs to *enable* interdependence to be identified easily. As the organisation develops and the continuous improvement tasks become more challenging, so the employees will become more demanding in their desire to develop new skills. Here you must be on your guard to ensure that training and development does have a foundation in the future needs of the organisation and it is not just training for training's sake.

During the development of an implementation plan (discussed in chapter 2), you will need consider the requirements for awareness training both in terms of preparing everyone for a total quality culture and preparing the managers to drive continuous improvement. However, to address the other continuing need, to develop a *training and development culture,* it is worthwhile investigating the Investors In People programme through your local Training and Enterprise Council (TEC).

INVESTING IN PEOPLE

The Investors In People programme sits well with any initiative aimed at developing a world class organisation because it is designed to focus attention on developing a *training and development culture.* This is based on 'setting and communicating business goals; developing people to meet these goals so that what people can do and are motivated to do matches what the business needs them to do'. Sounds familiar, doesn't it?

At the centre of the programme is a national standard, giving public recognition to the work an organisation has put into developing its people.

The programme commences with a survey of all members of staff, the results of which are interpreted against the four principles of Investors In People: *commitment, planning, action* and *evaluation*. The results from this survey can provide additional insight into the work needed to change the organisation's culture and where it should perhaps be most concentrated. The planning required for a training and development plan to introduce a total quality culture meets the requirements of Investors In People.

DEVELOPING MANAGERS

Introducing a total quality culture puts considerable strain on the management skills of both the senior team and the middle managers and supervisors. If they have been developed or simply 'picked up' informally they can be found wanting at a very early stage. Even if they have been developed through formal training and development programmes, they can also be found not to meet the new situation if they have been taught and developed in an inflexible, traditional, style.

The key skills that the managers and supervisors will be called upon to use, in a new application are:

- time management;
- communications;
- human relations and teamwork;
- effective meeting skills;
- solving problems and making decisions;
- leadership;
- motivation and getting the best out of people.

Time management

The time pressures of carrying out the implementation programme whilst still coping with business as usual with all its associated firefighting will be considerable in its early stages. The quotation '...be ruthless with time but gracious with people.' must be followed at all times. Being available to encourage activities, to brief and to debrief individuals on awareness training, to facilitate project groups and to prioritise fairly between the needs of the changing culture and the daily interaction with external customers and suppliers will require highly-developed time management awareness and skills.

Figure 4.1 provides a quick check on time management attitude and practice. It should be used initially to establish skill development needs and at regular intervals to measure practice development progress.

As a potential leader of the cultural change programme you must expect to be put under considerable time pressures as you come to terms with the commitment required to achieve permanent changes. You will need to be extremely effective in the way you manage your time as a further example to others around you.

However, before it is possible to improve your ability to manage your time more effectively, it is important that you have a clearer understanding of your own current attitude towards managing time and some of the basic issues and principles underlying good Practice.

To be a good manager of time you must be able to:

● prioritise clearly;

● make good decisions;

● plan your time effectively;

● delelegate and empower people;

● organise your work and that of other people effectively.

Managing my time	Agree	Disagree	No feelings either way
1. In managing time, it is usually best to work on the urgent problems immediately.			
2. It is always an indication of poor time management if a manager has lots of work in the evening and at weekends.			
3. While weekly or even monthly planning is essential for effective management of time it is not essential for managers to prepare daily plans for themselves.			
4. Top priority should usually be given to projects which help the accomplishment of other projects further down on the priority list because that will make tomorrow's time management easier.			
5. Setting tight but seemingly realistic deadlines is usually not a good technique since interruptions have a tendency to make these deadlines difficult to achieve.			
6. Doing one specific task at a time and finishing it before moving on to the next one is a good way to save time.			

Fig 4.1 Checklist for time management practice and skills

Managing my time	Agree	Disagree	No feelings either way
7. One of the best ways of making more time available is by saying 'no' and not getting personally involved in many of the problems that can properly be ignored, postponed or delegated.			
8. The most, difficult tasks, the ones requiring the most 'thinking' and analysis (like analysis of labour costs or performance appraisals), should be done early in the morning.			
9. All decisions and projects should be set into priority order and worked on in that order so that the things that are not completed are the ones with least priority.			
10. Executives at higher levels in an organisation waste much less time than do managers and supervisors at lower levels.			
11. Even though a manager's day brings many situations that cannot be anticipated, a specific written list of 'things that must be done today' is essential.			
12. Generally, things that are urgent should take precedence over matters that are important but not urgent.			
13. High priority should usually be given to those tasks which are very small and can therefore be accomplished quickly.			
14. The most important thing in effective time management is good priority setting.			

How did you do?

As you review your scores and the reasons for them, please remember they cannot be 'right' for every situation. The purpose of this checklist is to stimulate thought about the way you behave and to initiate change. Measure your success not in terms of the raw scores, but in terms of the new ideas you get and effectively put into practice, as measured by successive uses of the checklist. In the scoring having no opinion counts for zero as it will stimulate no debate in your own mind or with others.

Fig 4.1 Contd.

How did you do?	Agree	Disagree	No feelings either way
1. For effective management of time, urgent matters should always be evaluated, some should be done, some postponed and some ignored, but only if they are unimportant.	1	2	0
2. Working in the evenings or at weekends at times may not be a sign of poor management since a manager's workload may be very heavy for a limited period of time. If, on the other hand, a manager consistently puts in considerably more time than managers in similar positions, then it is probably either an indication that time is being poorly utilised or the manager is striving for exceptionally high achievement.	1	2	0
3. Daily plans are always useful. They are essential only, though, if a great many tasks have to be performed on a specific day. if there are relatively few things to be remembered, such detailed plans are not essential and of themselves waste time.	1	2	0
4. If a project helps toward the completion of another project, then it should be given higher priority than it would be on the basis of its own relative importance and urgency. That does not necessarily mean, though, that it should be given top priority. That would depend on how important and urgent it is.	1	2	0
5. Setting tight deadlines does not have to lead to superficial treatment of projects nor to excessive pressure to achieve deadlines. The challenging aspect of a tight deadline can be very beneficial in helping accomplish a job on time.	1	2	0
6. Rarely is it possible to finish a task of significant size at one time, without doing other things at the same time. However, to the extent to which that is possible, particularly with tasks that do not require considerable time, it is good practice.	2	1	0
7. This statement is correct. Wherever possible, matters which need not be handled by you should be delegated, ignored or postponed.	2	1	0

Fig 4.1 Contd.

How did you do?	Agree	Disagree	No feelings either way
8. There is no universal pattern for the 'best' time during the day for the manager to handle the more difficult tasks. Some managers like to do this type of work early in the morning; some find the afternoons the best; others prefer to do it in the evening. The most important thing, of course, is to determine what time during the day is 'best' for you and to use that information to your advantage in planning your daily tasks.	1	2	0
9. While it is certainly desirable that all decisions and projects be set into priority order, they very often cannot be worked on in that order. For example, a high priority matter can be delayed by influences beyond the manager's control and therefore need not be a top preference immediately. There are also urgent interruptions which can prompt a complete revamping of the priority list. However, despite these things, generally it is good practice to adhere to this rule of thumb.	2	1	0
10. Higher level managers usually have more opportunities for appropriate delegation and therefore have better control over how they would like to spend their time. This, however, does not mean that, on balance, they manage their time better.	1	2	0
11. As mentioned earlier, a specific list of things that must be done during the day is an extremely effective method of managing time. It helps assure that the most urgent and important tasks are completed daily.	2	1	0
12. Only to a limited extent should things that are urgent take preference over matters that are important, but not urgent. This issue is the very reason why frequently unimportant, but urgent, matters do seem to be given preference and, as a result, some important matters are postponed until they become urgent; then crises usually develop.	1	2	0
13. High priority should only be given to those small tasks which are also important in addition to being urgent. Temptations are great to work on simple things and those things which are easy to accomplish, but these temptations should be resisted. It is usually a good idea to keep a running list of all tasks so that they can take their appropriate place in the priority list and not be overlooked.	1	2	0

Fig 4.1 contd.

How did you do?	Agree	Disagree	No feelings either way
14. Setting priorities is the most important activity in effective personal time management because all decisions pertaining to time management are, in essence, decisions which assign priorities. This holds true when managers accept or reject interruptions as well as when they decide which tasks to do immediately and which to postpone.	2	0	0
TOTAL SCORES			

Fig 4.1 contd.

Communications

When starting out on a new initiative people need to have continuous communication of the right kind. The communication needs to be two-way. It must be regular, clear and reliable. Let us consider for a moment the definition of communication:

a two-way process (or exchange) to create understanding in the minds of others in order to promote action.

Exactly what is required to create cultural change? *Action.*

Communication can be in many forms but in the early stages of the implementation it must be mostly based on face-to-face communication during which trust and rapport can be established. Feedback is an important element of communication. It demonstrates understanding and commitment especially when the feedback is the result of a return communication *up* the organisational structure. Checking for understanding and soliciting feedback is a role model habit.

Where managers and supervisors are not natural communicators, they will have to develop the habit quickly, giving it priority. Teams which do not receive regular verbal communication are soon left behind, becoming resentful of the programme and of their supervisors. They are quickly seen as blockers and barriers to change.

Whilst communications is one of the environmental issues that will be the subject of a formal policy to ensure regular communication, this in itself will not be enough. Good communications skills, actively employed daily by supervisors and managers prevent blocks occurring and create the right environment for trust to grow.

A number of organisations bidding to become world class have successfully trained all of their employees to have good presentation skills as an early part of their culture change programme. Much of their business is built on being open with their external customers and encouraging regular factory visits. Having employees who are trained to make presentations means that the whole workforce can be involved with customers, not just sales and marketing departments. This creates an environment which is truly customer-focused and where there are fewer opportunities for barriers to be created.

From personal experience of visiting these organisations, the whole atmosphere is more open and friendly and one has a sense of '... come and ask me what I am doing ...' This contrasts with an attitude of '... don't look at what I am doing' which comes across when touring organisations where people are not confident when talking about what they do, because communication is not seen as a key skill for them.

Where are your managers and supervisors with regard to having good communication skills? Use Figure 4.2 as a checklist to find out.

Human relations and teamwork

The biggest and often most difficult transition the managers and supervisors must make during the early implementation of total quality management is that of the role change from 'cop' to 'coach'. There is little place within a world class organisation for the 'controlling and directive' management style designed to provide maximum support to the managers themselves. The style required to make a total quality culture work and develop into a world class one is that of 'empowering and enabling' designed to support the subordinate and to get the best from them by encouraging them to participate and to use their total brain power as a company resource. This change starts with listening to, involving and empathising with individuals. It develops into helping them to help themselves and to become more confident in doing things for themselves. And allowing them to make mistakes and to learn from them rather than to be admonished for making them out of ignorance.

Developing a new relationship with workers who hitherto have never been involved, always directed, is not easy, nor is the creation of the feeling of being part of a team when previously it has always been a case of looking after 'number one', i.e. yourself.

Having an awareness of the different traits, tendencies and characteristics individuals may possess and the way these interact to make the whole individual is an important start point, because people will remain individuals however differently they are treated. Just as we all have different likes and

	Seldom	Sometimes	Always
1. I always listen to other people's views before stating my own.			
2. In meetings we always listen to each other and never talk over the person who is talking.			
3. I am always open and honest with others. I never keep information back that is relevant to the discussion.			
4. I can always be persuaded by fair argument to help achieve consensus.			
5. I believe those who are physically the biggest and talk the loudest get their own way.			
6. I regularly publish and explain departmental performance details to my staff.			
7. I provide and explain details of the organisation's financial performance, targets and goals to my staff.			
8. I believe in encouraging employees to discuss problems openly.			
9. I encourage staff to question senior management on all aspects of the organisation's operations and policies and ensure answers are provided to their questions promptly.			
10. I am effective at communicating changes to everyone who is involved or who will be affected by the changes.			
11. I never feed or listen to the 'grapevine'.			
12. I always listen to people with difficulties and support and counsel them as appropriate.			
Now identify areas of weakness and develop action plans to improve your performance where you have not ticked 'always'.			

Fig 4.2 Checklist for communication skills

dislikes when it comes to food or holidays, so we all have different prefer-ences for the way we participate in work problems, the way we work in teams, the way we approach problems and the way we see change. These facets are dealt with in more detail in chapter 8 on teamwork. However, at this point you should be planning help, in the form of training, for managers and supervisors to maximise their effect in changing the way they work with people by understanding them better and valuing their differences.

Understanding people's needs when it comes to working in a team, leading teams to enable them to be creative and not imposing management will on them are other areas which must be addressed. Managing team resources to spread the involvement; using key people as team facilitators in order to share the load, and maintaining a common, systematic approach, to creating and using teamwork will put further pressure on management and supervisor skills and competencies.

Effective meeting skills

One could consider effective meeting skills as one of the key skills of time management, which of course it is. However, in the context of successfully implementing the introduction of total quality management effective meeting skills warrants a place of its own.

Communicating, sharing, discussing, involving, solving problems and improving processes all require meetings. If the skills within the organisation to organise and to operate meetings effectively are found wanting there will be no time left for the organisation to fulfil its proper tasks. There will be lots of meetings, especially in the early stages of the implementation. These must be short and effective. Meetings do not solve problems, only actions in the form of assignments can achieve that, but meetings are essential for sharing information, discussing the way forward and agreeing actions.

Effective meeting skills can be learned and developed by everybody but initially they must be demonstrated by the senior and middle managers and supervisors.

Solving problems and making decisions

The regular use of the tools of total quality, described in chapter 12, and their employment in a systematic way by the managers and supervisors within an organisation is vital in setting the standard and demonstrating a commitment to their use throughout the organisation. Traditionally, problems have been solved by managers in a somewhat cloak and dagger way from the view point of the workforce, who have seldom had any involvement.

	Seldom	Sometimes	Always
1. I provide support and directions to my staff as appropriate to their proven competence.			
2. I discuss changes to operating systems and proceedures with my staff before any descision is made to implement change.			
3. When faced with a problem I establish a team to work on it comprising the people who carry out the process or activity.			
4. When establishing a team I do not consider the individuals' team suitability, only their appropriateness to the successful completion of the task.			
5. The first task of any team, afler agreeing clear objectives, is to consider the strengths and weaknesses of the team and the individuals that make it up in order to plan the work together in a sytematic and orderly fashion valuing differences and using strengths as a major resource.			
6. I rarely if ever impose my will on the team.			
7. I adopt a coaching, teaching and skill-enhancing role towards my staff and teams with which I am associated.			
8. I regularly set time aside to discuss individual performance and improvement needs with individual members of my team.			
9. I encourage the use of the systematic quality improvement cycle and quality tools in teams and their use by individuals in their daily roles.			
10. All team members and individuals within my remit recieve regular reward and recognition for their efforts to create a quality environment of continuous improvement.			

Where you have ticked 'seldom' consider what actions you could take to change your behaviour before you become a block to the progress of your organisation's TQ implementation plan.

If you have ticked 'sometimes' consider how you can be more consistent in your behaviour to prevent giving mixed signals to your staff.

Fig 4.3 Checklist for human relationships and teamwork

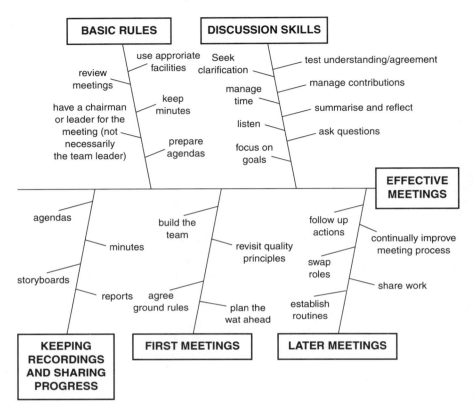

Fig 4.4 Checklist for effective meeting skills

Often the methodology used relies more on experience than a systematic approach, using gut feel or experience rather than facts. In the past the route to solving problems has been a short one from symptom (or effect) to solution with little regard for the real, root cause of the problem.

Such approaches have permitted some 'high flying' executives to make a career out of their expertise at 'solving' the same problem over and over again in many different organisations, moving on from company to company as their reputation for problem solving has grown. Unfortunately, it has been all too often the case that the problems have returned later. The short track approach from symptom to solution results in a papering over of the cracks, to open up again later, again and again.

The only acceptable approach in a world class organisation is a systematic one which takes a steady journey from symptom to cause to root to permanent solution, using facts, not opinions.

Most managers have had little formal training in good methods of problem-solving and decision-making which will make this change in their behaviour difficult. Where it is absent, particular attention to good methods should be included in the initial total quality management awareness training.

	Agree	Sometimes	Disagree
1. When confronted with a problem I use my experience of similar situations to develop a solution.			
2. I always consider all the alternatives presented to me before making up my mind.			
3. I take care to evaluate all of the possibilities to ensure that when I make a decision it will meet my objectives.			
4. Systematic approaches to problem-solving are the only proper way to solve problems.			
5. Taking time to identify the root cause of a problem and taking steps to eliminate it is always worthwhile.			
6. When I make a decision it really only matters that the needs of my department and in particular my policies are met.			
7. I have one decision-making style and stick to it as I can rely on the results.			
8. It is important to take time to understand a problem thoroughly before attempting to build a solution.			
9. Using teams to solve urgent problems takes too long. It is better for a manager to solve these alone.			
10. Before implementing a decision I take great care to identify potential problems and barriers and look to overcome them within the implementation plan.			

Fig 4.5 Checklist for solving problems and making decisions

How did you do?

To check your approach to problem-solving and decision-making and its compatibility with a total quality approach, ring the score appropriate to your answer and total the scores at the bottom of the table.

Scores	Agree	Sometimes	Disagree
1.	0	1	2
2.	2	1	0
3.	2	1	0
4.	2	1	0
5.	2	1	0
6.	0	0	2
7.	0	0	2
8.	2	1	0
9.	0	1	2
10.	2	1	0
Total score			

If your score is between:

16–20 Your approach to problem-solving and decision-making is compatible with that of a TQ approach and you should be able to exhibit role model behaviour in this vital area.

11–15 You still have a little of the traditionalist about you and may need to kerb your natural leadership tendencies and shepherd people along more, rather than setting the pace and asking people to follow. You must be careful not to be papering over the cracks.

6–10 You are operating in a very traditional manner that is likely to give mixed and confusing signals to your subordinates. Study the plan–do–check–act approach and consider being positive in your involvement of others and listening to their ideas.

0–5 Start listening and learning or it is you that will be the problem to be solved.

Fig 4.5 contd.

Leadership

Initially, the traditional 'lead from the front and the others follow' style is wanted, showing the way by example. However, as the programme takes hold the style must change subtly to one of shepherding, encouraging from behind, supporting change and being the first to adopt new ways of doing things. This still means showing by example, but more the setting an example rather than previously leading by it.

It is important to understand your own leadership style at the outset so that you can plan how far and how quickly to change. As we discussed earlier when considering human relationships and teamwork the change is one from the 'controlling and directive' style to an 'empowering and enabling' style.

Different organisations and the different functions and sections within them require different leadership styles and methods of exercising power. They are dependent on situation, level of development and maturity. Good leaders will have developed a range of styles which are used in different circumstances and situations. They will demonstrate above-average skill in developing warm relationships with their working groups and in initiating new ways to solve problems. They will have come to terms with the role conflict between getting work out and promoting good interpersonal relationships. Generally speaking, there are four well-defined power strategies.

Boss power

This assumes that people need to be told what to do. Users of this strategy tend to stress the need to control people, believing that they are motivated primarily by external factors and cannot be trusted to be self-motivated. 'Boss powered' people, therefore, believe that other people depend on them.

This style is more frequently found today in small organisations, often new ones undergoing fast development and growth, run somewhat autocratically by self-made entrepreneurs who find it difficult to lead in any other way. It can however still be found in larger organisations which believe they have changed. Beware.

System power

System power uses similar assumptions to 'boss power' except that in this case the influencing is done via policies, procedures, regulations and rules. Again, the assumption is that getting people to do what is required is a question of telling them – but this time through prescribed systems.

Users of this style try to hide behind a faceless bureaucracy rather than own up to giving directives. The style is found widely in more mature organisations, such as civil service and, local government. These organisations, may espouse the ethos of quality assurance through the attainment of ISO 9000 registration but use the system only as a means of imposing directives.

Peer power

Peer power places emphasis on influencing people through a strategy of being considerate and getting on well with them. 'Peer power' people will argue that you get your way with people by being skilled in interpersonal behaviour, being empathetic and sensitive, and being liked or respected by them. A peer-powered person needs to be popular and to receive approval and respect from other people.

This style can be found in many organisations already and is seen to work well. It is however often seen as weak-minded leadership by those who favour the use of boss power and those who favour it but use system power. Those who favour peer power are likely to be successful in making the total quality culture change work. However, they will need more steel at the outset when a mixture of boss power, in terms of decisiveness, and peer power, in terms of listening, will be needed.

Goal power

Goal power makes the assumption that people will show self-direction and self-control and in effect will influence themselves in actioning objectives to which they are committed. The goal-powered person is therefore keen to set and agree goals with people and then trust them to behave appropriately within the boundaries set by the goals or objectives. The goal power strategy also assumes that it is possible to achieve harmony between organisational goals and personal goals.

The goal power style is obviously the one which is required of a world class organisation. It embraces the assumptions of total quality and is supported by the cascade of the organisational goals into the sections and ultimately to the individual.

Leadership styles which couple with the power styles are traditionally known as:

- autocratic;
- bureaucratic;
- charismatic;
- democratic;
- laissez-faire.

Effective leadership depends on a multitude of conditions. There is no predetermined correct way to behave as a leader. The choice of leadership patterns should be based upon an accurate diagnosis of the reality of the situation in which the leader is placed.

As the implementation programme progresses this diagnosis will need to be more and more accurate and sensitive. Again, managers and supervisors will need to develop new skills in the exercising of power together with a lot of listening, trust and openness. As with the other skills these will develop as you actively support the environment, thus creating enablers by using the new policies and methods visibly throughout your work.

	Agree	Sometimes	Disagree
1. I always delegate work and authority across broad tasks and objectives.			
2. I value the expertise and experience of my staff as a major part of realising the organisation's full potential.			
3. I encourage my staff to bring their problems to me to solve for them.			
4. I do not lay blame when things go wrong, I look on mistakes as learning opportunities for all involved.			
5. I do not encourage changes of role. It is better to maintain the continuity of fixed roles.			
6. I see it as a motivator of care in what people do to maintain an environment of uncertainty and insecurity.			
7. I see myself as guide and counsellor first and controller last.			
8. I try not to confuse staff with more information than is necessary to complete the immediate task			
9. I encourage individuals and teams to request resources as they are required and make them available if it is within my gift.			
10. I try to ensure that the most senior members lead project teams.			

Fig 4.6 Power users' checklist

How did you do?

To check your attitude to the exercise of the power of your position, ring the score appropriate to your answer and total the scores at the bottom of the table.

Scores	Agree	Sometimes	Disagree
1.	2	1	0
2.	2	1	0
3.	0	1	2
4.	2	1	0
5.	0	1	2
6.	0	0	2
7.	2	1	0
8.	0	1	2
9.	2	1	0
10.	0	0	2
Total score			

If your score is between:

16–20 You obviously believe in enabling, empowering and supporting your subordinates. This bodes well for successful cultural change.

11–15 You have probably found some people-focused activities pay dividends but are not totally convinced of the TQ approach. This may confuse your subordinates by giving out mixed messages if you do not try to be more empowering in your approach.

6–10 You are operating in a traditional manner that will probably lead to resentment and confusion on the part of subordinates during any attempts to change the culture of the organisation.

0–5 You are likely to be a major blocker of cultural change and need to take immediate and urgent action to change.

Fig 4.6 contd.

Motivation and getting the best out of people

A lot has been written about motivation but what is it?

Motivation is what makes a person want to do something; it is what makes them put energy and effort into what they do. Motivational energy can vary in nature and intensity between individuals depending on the particular influences on them at any given point in time. There are many factors which effect a individual's motivation:

- *past experience* upbringing, education, previous experiences at work;
- *present situation* needs at the present time, how colleagues are perceived;
- *perception of the future* perceived prospects in the organisation, perceived prospects outside the organisation.

Motivation is seen by the individual in terms of what rewards the organisation or the individual's manager or supervisor is able to offer. What do we know about motivation is that it is vital in any job if an individual is to give their best. Assuming that employees are given ample opportunity for good performance, correct tools, work methods, organisational structure, etc, and have the necessary skills, their effectiveness depends on their own motivation. Good motivation is certainly related to morale. It has a direct but casual relationship with productivity and staff that are properly motivated can be changed from a mediocre group into a highly productive team.

There are many and varied theories on motivation. The key figures in the field such as Douglas McGregor, Abraham Maslow, Frederick Herzberg and D F McClelland have changed their opinion on team dynamics over time. They all came to realise that groups are not the democratic entity that everyone would like them to be, but responded to individual, strong, well directed leadership both from *without* and *within* the group, just like individuals.

One of the earliest researchers was F W Taylor, whose studies showed that workers would respond to a wage incentive. He believed that increased wages more than offset any intrinsic loss of interest that workers might experience in their job over the years. Initial work by Elton Mayo with the Hawthorne experiments and McGregor with T-Groups were largely replaced by later work. Mayo emphasised the importance of the small work group in motivating workers. He felt that the social relationships of the employees assumed more importance than money.

McGregor, when he himself eventually became a manager (college president), formed his hypothesis that when a manager carried out his responsibilities he based his actions on a series of assumptions or theories, whether these be implicit or explicit. While there will clearly be many individual variations, he maintained that there are basically two theories about human nature used by managers in general. These he labelled Theory X and Theory Y.

Theory X is the manager's view of employees *needing* to be lead:

- The average human being has an inherent dislike of work and will avoid it if he can.
- Because of this human characteristic of dislike of work, most people must be coerced, controlled, directed and threatened with punishment to get them to put forth adequate effort toward the achievement of organisational objectives.
- The average human being prefers to be directed, wishes to avoid responsibility, has relatively little ambition, wants security above all.

Theory Y is the manager's view of employees wishing to be lead:

- The expenditure of physical and mental effort in work is as natural as play or rest.
- External control and the threat of punishment are not the only means for bringing about effort toward organisational objectives. Man will exercise self-direction and self-control in the service of objectives to which he is committed.
- Commitment to objectives is a function of the rewards associated with their achievement.
- The average human being learns, under proper conditions, not only to accept but to seek responsibility.
- The capacity to exercise a relatively high degree of imagination, ingenuity, and creativity in the solution or organisational problems is widely, not narrowly, distributed in the population.
- Under the conditions of modern industrial life, the intellectual potential of the average human being is only partly utilised.

Of course if you reverse the roles you get the same results.

The X approach reflects the paternalistic and mechanistic approaches to management; the Y approach is reflective of the participative style of management favoured in a world class organisation.

Abraham Maslow's contribution was to put needs that he felt existed into a hierarchical sequence and he postulated the theory that the lower level can emerge. His model is really that of self-actualising where the individual can realise their full potential and can create opportunities for themselves. He felt that management needed to address itself to that level of need if job performance was to be improved.

Later Professor Herzberg carried out investigations into the factors affecting job attitudes. Based on an analysis of his findings, he suggested that the things which lead to *dissatisfaction* are not equal and opposite. He labelled the satisfying factors as *motivators* and the dissatisfying factors as *hygiene factors*. They may be summarised as:

- *Hygiene needs* are how you are treated at work: salary, supervision, working conditions. These hygiene factors merely keep people from being unhappy; they do not motivate people.

- *Motivators are achievement, recognition for achievement, increased responsibility, growth and advancement at work.* However, to become motivated, people need *ability* (training) and the *opportunity* to use that ability. Job enrichment, feedback, self-checking, direct communication all aid the motivators, according to Herzberg. Herzberg concluded that when management said 'its my fault' – owning up to being not such capable managers, who made mistakes once in a while – then a new understanding (culture) would develop. The biggest problem in industry said Herzberg was creating the opportunity for people to use their abilities. All jobs should inherently be a learning experience and a growth experience.

What makes people happy and motivated at work is what they do. What makes people unhappy, is the situation in which they do it.

More recently, D F McClelland took a more selective view of motivation through the work he had done in trying to define achievement. He estimated that only one in ten of the population had strong achievement motivations. He identified achievers as:

- setting their own goals to which they committed themselves and for which they were fully responsible for attainment;
- wanting to win and therefore selecting a goal at which they know they can achieve;
- wanting positive and immediate feedback from the task.

McClelland's theory suggests that it is possible to build achievement characteristics into jobs such as:

- personal responsibility;
- individual participation in the selection of productivity targets;

- moderate goals;
- fast, clear-cut feedback.

As the theories have developed, they are to a large extent supportive of the needs of a world class culture and require skill development and a flexible approach by the managers and supervisors if the change is to be successfully met.

To get the most out of people, managers must:

- be approachable at all times;
- maintain credibility throughout;
- be capable of seeing the other person's point of view;
- take criticism and advice at all levels;
- set a high standard for themselves and their staff;
- generate and maintain enthusiasm for the task;
- let the team know what standards are expected of them and review performance regularly;
- think positively and transmit this attitude to the team;
- give praise when praise is due;
- handle mistakes in a positive and constructive manner.

Giving feedback and delegating are two further skills which aid motivation and getting the best out of people. These must be developed to meet the demands of the implementation plan. Figure 4.7 provides a checklist for how well you are motivating your staff.

Score each statement below on a scale one to ten. One being 'no, not at all', and 10 being 'yes, very definitely'. Try to be as honest as you can. Nobody else will see the answers. They will be used by you to improve the effectiveness of your team.

*   I know my staff very well on an individual basis.   _____

*   I know what motivates my staff on an individual basis
both inside and outside the work situation.   _____

*   I check out the above regularly.

*   I offer my staff challenging opportunities without asking them   _____
to exceed their abilities.

*   I use my staff's strengths to the full and work with them to   _____
eliminate their weaknesses.

Fig 4.7 How well are you motivating your staff?

* I offer my staff learning opportunities and coach them
to develop them in the job. _____

* I give immediate recognition for a job well done. _____

* I give regular feedback to my staff on their performance
and not leave it only to annual appraisals. _____

* I tell my colleagues how well my team is doing. _____

* I make every attempt to ensure my staff get all the rewards
to which they are entitled. _____

* I delegate truly interesting parts of my iob and not just the trivia. _____

* I involve my team in as much joint decision-making as is
practically possible. _____

* I hold regular creativity sessions with my team to identify
and solve work-related problems. _____

* I hold regular meetings to give information to my staff. _____

* My staff are completely clear on the team objective and
their contribution to it. _____

* My staff understand that they have a responsibility to
approach their work with a positive attitude – and they do. _____

Fig 4.7 contd.

5

Communicating Your Plan to All

If you don't tell them what you want, they cannot follow or maintain the momentum

- **Planning to launch the programme of change**
- **Rehearsal**
- **Actions and activities that maintain the momentum**
- **Eliminate the us and them syndrome**

INTRODUCTION

So far we have discussed the overall picture of what constitutes a world class organisation planning; how to make it happen in your organisation; and the important part managers will play in implementing of a programme for change through their behaviour and skills. Now we have come to the first real *actions*.

At some point, the organisation has to announce its intentions to the employees at large. During the preparation and planning phase a lot of interest will have been aroused, expectations created and possibly some entrenched positions of hostility may have been taken up. The time has arrived to reveal the plan. This is a critical stage. If you hit the right note the programme will be off to a flying start; get it wrong and it will be consigned to the waste bin by the company cynics together with all those other initiatives from previous years.

Here are a number of important guidelines:

- the plan must be communicated as something special and different to anything that has been done or attempted before;
- it must be seen as something that will last for a long time, not put over as this year's special effort;
- the initial communication meets a need to know what is happening; has an atmosphere of change about it; and has been built up beforehand by careful internal marketing;

- everyone must receive the same input over as short a time scale as is practical to beat the grapevine, or the impact of the message will be lost;
- it must be planned carefully and executed with a high degree of professionalism (that is not to imply that it must be a grand, stage-managed affair with high levels of audiovisual input, if that is not your organisation's culture, but it has to make an impact).

PLANNING THE LAUNCH

What are the activities necessary to put a launch together?

The venue and date

Once dates and the venue are agreed, the launch is booked at the agreed venue even if it is internal, outlining the layout and equipment requirements.

What will be said?

When it comes to what will be said, who will say it and what material will be needed, the issues which are to be addressed are:

- the purpose of the programme, i.e. establish a need;
- will you want to use a video to show the art of the possible?
- the organisation mission statement, objectives and improvement goals explained;
- communicate key messages from any surveys that have been conducted, *customer*, *supplier* and *employee*;
- outline the plan for the training cascade and the timetable for establishing the 'top down' teams;
- outline the policies to be introduced to change the environment in which people work together, with target dates for full introduction;
- who will present each element?
- is it to be fully scripted and agreed?
- what slides and visuals will be needed?
- how will the event be marked (badges, pens, mugs, pads, give-aways)?

Additional material requirements are identified to complete the company launch package and individual speakers are briefed.

The communication cascade

Trying to maintain the impact over a large number of presentations is difficult and wherever possible the launch should be done in the fewest number of events. Shift patterns, if worked, will make this difficult. However, experience suggests that more difficulty is found in launching to too few at a time over an extended period, than across shifts where there is little time for the 'grapevine' to take over.

When planning who will attend and when, it must be borne in mind that the preferred grouping for such an important launch is to take a full mix of people from up, down and across the organisation. In this way, a whole company team approach is adopted from the start.

Advising managers

People must be available to attend at the time they have been invited. To achieve this, each manager should be appraised of the launch arrangements carefully and given time to plan how the people will be released at the time required.

Developing a promotional pack

The idea of internal promotion and internal marketing may be new to you and you may think it has no place in your organisation's culture. However, some degree of internal promotion is vital to establish the right level of anticipation before the launch. Where it is already part of your culture, then you must consider carefully the level. This must not be seen as yet another communication, it has to be different. You may decide, if you have not already done so, to give the programme a name or a title. This may be only for internal consumption, but nevertheless something that will give the programme life, identity and a personality.

A key element of any pre-launch publicity must be a personal invitation from the chief executive to every employee, at whatever level, full or part time, permanent or temporary. Some organisations favour a teasing poster campaign; others carry out special briefings using either existing or newly-formed briefing groups (using briefing groups for the first time instead of the company noticeboard does make the build-up special); others send out low-key letters with the invitations. Whatever you choose, it should be special for your organisation. The important thing is that, whether high profile or low key, it must be different to anything you have done before.

Rehearse the speakers

With the promotional activity underway and the presentation material prepared, the speakers must rehearse. *This is not an optional activity.* We discussed earlier in this chapter the need to make the launch special and for it to be 'professional' as far as possible. That does not mean a highly-developed audiovisual presentation, it means good presentation skills, good timing, slick, people demonstrating a high degree of professionalism. Yes, presentation aids can augment a good presentation, but they will not make up for a poorly-rehearsed performance.

There is an expression used often in training circles: 'Amateurs practise until they get it right, professionals practise until they cannot get it wrong.' If you want to deliver a slick, well-timed, word perfect presentation, the speakers must practise until they cannot get it wrong. Simply, they must practise on their own until they get it right. Speaking into a mirror helps get the pacing right and the expressions, arm movements and the like. People who have difficulty reading from a prepared script need to practise even more, using ever-reducing levels of notes until they can use only the visual aids as headlines and prompts.

Once this level of expertise has been achieved, it is time to try it out in the venue whenever possible (certainly a final rehearsal should take place there), with all speakers together to ensure continuity of content and messages. Timings should be made throughout to ensure that the launch presentation itself stays on time. Role model behaviour from the start.

MAINTAINING THE MOMENTUM

Once the launch has been completed, even if the awareness training starts immediately, there is likely to be a hiatus. Thus must be filled with meaningful activity, demonstrating that things are changing for the better and that the launch was not just good, but empty, words.

Again we are saying *visible actions* are required.

As soon as a few people in each section have been trained, or at least have a new level of awareness, middle managers, supervisors and team leaders can take positive action to reinforce the messages about becoming customer-focused and process-oriented. This can be done by starting to map the processes of the function, section or department and carrying out a formal *process analysis* (see chapter 12).

Once established, process maps or flowcharts can be used for many purposes; identifying customers and suppliers within a process; establishing formal procedures by agreeing a common way of performing the same task, irrespective of function or department; training newcomers to the team or section; helping create awareness of what you do in other functions, and of course improving the process by finding new methods. In addition, the team leader can start using *team purpose analysis* and *departmental purpose analysis* (see chapter 12). These both involve the use of process maps. These activities are very visible and participative, involving team members in tasks that reinforce the messages from their training in a practical way. They can open the way quickly to improved performance, reduced waste and shorter cycle times.

ELIMINATING THE 'US AND THEM' SYNDROME

Grand gestures immediately following the launch are often counter-productive if they are not maintained, but saving one or two things which could have been introduced earlier is not a bad thing, especially if they are aimed at reducing the 'us and them' syndrome. Some organisations start to develop an egalitarian regime by eliminating special parking areas for managers, including the chief executive and the chairman, keeping special areas for visitors and customers only.

There is an NHS trust hospital near to my home in Derbyshire that insists it is customer-focused and is dedicated to providing 'quality service' to the community. However, anxious visitors looking for a parking space are faced with one which is almost always empty but has a sign by it which says 'space reserved at all times for trust chair'. Who is more important here? Where is the customer focus? Such things destroy an image and a reputation very quickly and say to people – 'we don't really mean what we say.'

Other organisations favour a common uniform and introduce it as a first move after the launch of their programme. This can help break down the barriers, but the danger is that some executives will bring the programme into disrepute before it has had time to get started, by making themselves out to be different. This can happen even if the chief executive wears the uniform fastidiously.

There are many areas where little actions can demonstrate the commitment, such as establishing noticeboards which are kept up-to-date, fresh and relevant by assigning people to be responsible for the board. Using team purpose analysis also starts the process of establishing team and individual goals as well as objectives and improvement targets. Frequent news sheets whilst the awareness training is being undertaken keeps up the momentum in terms of news dissemination, as do special additions as the first improvement project teams are established, publicising team membership and where they can be located.

Once again the emphasis is on *visible actions*.

Figure 5.1 gives a checklist for the launch.

1 Agree date and venue	☐
2 Book venue	☐
• **Equipment.**	☐
• **Food and drinks if required.**	☐
• **Accommodation for VIPs (if required).**	☐
3 Plan communication cascade	☐

Issues to be addressed are:

- the use of the standard set slides;
- the use of a TQ video;
- additional material required to communicate, including key points from any surveys and data gathering exercises;
- integration of standard material and additional materials;
- the number of sessions required;
- individual speakers;
- briefings for individual speakers.

4 Advise managers of arrangements	☐
5 Develop additional material	☐
6 Promote launch	☐
7 Rehearse speakers	☐
8 Review all requirements for launch	☐

Fig 5.1 Launch preparation checklist

6

Getting off to a Fast Start

Giving the initial awareness training a chance in creating a process-oriented culture

- **The key role of pre- and post-training briefing**
- **Capturing all of the ideas – good and bad**
- **A project management system to avoid the activity trap**
- **Using all resources evenly**
- **The value of trained facilitators**

INTRODUCTION

The cascade of awareness training will inevitably create a level of expectation regarding being talked to, consulted, listened to and generally involved as never before. Participants in the sessions will come away with a whole host of good ideas (in their opinion) as to how the organisation can be improved, if only they are listened to. The expectations must be met and people's good ideas must be captured and, where possible, acted upon. At the same time, the situation must be managed positively, constructively and effectively. It is all too easy to appear negative as you still try to manage 'business as usual' and to fall into what is known widely as the *activity trap* where through trying too hard to listen, take action and involve people, so much is going on that 'business as usual' almost gets forgotten – and the external customers too.

To achieve all the desired positive outcomes and make a fast but controlled start, avoiding the activity traps, you need to address three issues and develop firm methods to be followed:

- Establish formal pre- and post-course briefing for all participants by their direct supervisor.
- Establish a formal system for collecting good ideas and opportunities for improvement and for managing and monitoring the action taken on

them. Keep focused on the needs of the business and the established improvement goals.

- Establish methods to monitor individuals involved in the improvement process and ensure that positive discrimination is exercised in the assembly of new teams to maximise the opportunity to involve everybody in the improvement process.

PRE- AND POST-COURSE BRIEFINGS

The actual purpose of the awareness training is to provide the participants, the individual employees of the organisation, with the knowledge, skills, confidence and enthusiasm to enable them to participate fully in the programme of change by applying and using the principles of total quality and the tools to improve their everyday work. To ensure that this investment in training is converted swiftly into co-ordinated and effective action requires a formal process operated by all managers and supervisors.

Briefing before training

Following the launch process there will be a variety of interpretations of what is going to happen. Before the individual undertakes the awareness training there is a requirement to ensure that they enter the training with a common understanding of what will happen and the objectives. In a large organisation, awareness training is likely to take weeks or even months. During that time, memories of the launch will dim and the logistics of filling courses, providing cover for people being trained, avoiding holidays and the occasional absence from work may become preoccupying.

A process of explaining the purpose of the training and how it will benefit the individual afterwards is essential. It is good practice to book a date and time for the briefing when the individual is given the date for training. In the briefing the supervisor should try to include the following:

- Clarify the joining instructions in terms of the date, time, place, travel arrangements, personal situation regarding finishing times, etc. (*It is vital that the participant feels comfortable with the experience.*) Explain and agree the arrangements for cover for the individual (if applicable) whilst on the course.
- Review the messages from the launch and remind the individual of the organisation's mission to become world class.
- Remind them, if necessary, that everyone is sharing the same training experience and why.

- Explain that management does not have a monopoly on good ideas and that it is only by tapping into the minds and creativity of all employees that the organisation will achieve its declared world class goals.
- The training will provide an opportunity to develop individual action plans for improvement as well as provide opportunities for identifying ways in which the organisation can improve the way it operates.
- Explain the 'top down' improvement activity already in place or planned and those teams that have started up as a result of the training already and those planned which may involve that individual (if appropriate).
- Agree a date for the follow-up debriefing.
- Ensure any further concerns the individual still has are fully answered.

After the training

As the participants leave their training they will be asking 'what now?' The debriefing is to ensure that the energy and enthusiasm resulting from the training is quickly converted into action. To achieve this your procedure should include:

- Discussion about how the participant found the course; reaction to the overall programme; and any concerns on its application to the function or team.
- Review of the individual's action plan developed during the course. Offer time to help develop ideas further and to carry the plan forward.
- Discuss any opportunities for improvement identified and agree how they can be acted upon.
- Explain again how the individual will become involved in improvement teams and will be helped to apply the tools.
- Explain how to raise issues of poor internal customer service, further ideas for opportunities for improvement and to discuss blockages and barriers which remain.

In chapter 4 management styles were discussed and the need for of a style which is seen and felt to be supportive, encouraging and enthusiastic for the new culture. It is important that this is the style in which the pre- and post-course briefings are carried out. This will signal the change in behaviour really has started, which is vital to maximising the benefit from the awareness training and the speed with which it is transformed into action. To achieve this, line managers, supervisors and team leaders must prepare thoroughly, planning time to carry through the briefings completely with everyone and developing the correct style with its mixture of coach, listener, enabler and challenger of the status quo.

A PROJECT MANAGEMENT SYSTEM

An important part of the preparation for implementation is the development of a system to capture the good ideas and manage them through to implementation in a timely and focused way. Maintaining sight of the priorities of the business as well as the need to empower. Any system you develop must be able to integrate the control of the 'top down' projects, the major improvement initiatives of the programme, with the easy collection and recording of 'bottom up' ideas and control their simply being acted upon or conversion into major 'bottom up' projects. A project management system of this type will have a number of different types of customer, some of whose requirements may well be in conflict. A poorly-designed system can easily alienate its customers and become ineffective. The system will fail if people do not understand what they are doing and why. They fail as well if people do not own that part of the process for which they are responsible, so the task of designing a suitable system is not just a technical matter; people issues are important too.

Let us examine the key requirements of such a system. The system must be able to track and demonstrate via regular reports progress achieved in terms of:

- number of ideas generated;
- number of improvement teams;
- number of active projects;
- number and names of employees involved in improvement teams;
- stage within the Deming PDCA quality cycle of each team (chapter 9);
- time spent on project work;
- project benefits;
- project costs.

Access to the system must be easy for everyone (ownership and empowerment), not necessarily through a supervisor. Figure 6.1 shows an outline for a project management system.

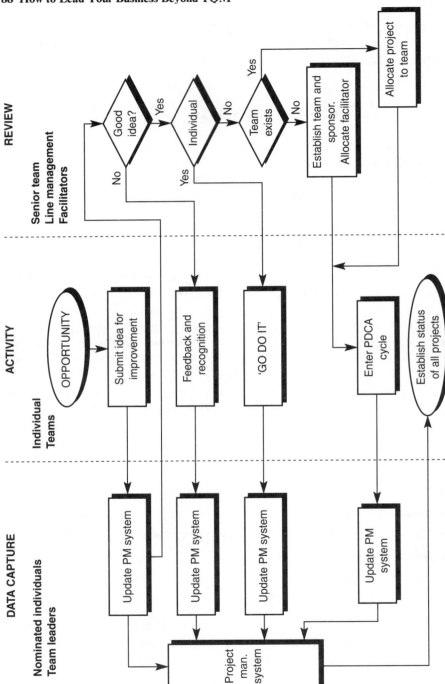

Fig 6.1 Outline project management (PM) system

USING RESOURCES EFFECTIVELY

Finally, in getting off to a good start, we turn our attention to setting up the improvement teams. The 'top down' teams, set up to achieve the key improvement targets set in the company workshop at the start of the programme, will have been set up already and they should have followed the same process. When setting up improvement teams, it is not a question of who will make the best team member, because everyone who joins a team must have something to contribute. They must be part of the process and to some extent know about or be effected by the problem.

The correct way to approach the establishment of an improvement team, at whatever level, is from the process view. The first step therefore is to map the process as a flow chart, or the part of the process where the problem is suspected to be. This will provide sight of the people involved in the process, who are likely to know something about the problem.

If we look at Figure 6.2 and imagine there is a big problem (or being positive as, we should be, an opportunity for improvement) which effects mainly Department B, such is the interdependence of departments within processes, that Department A knows something of the problem, so do Departments C and D to a lesser extent. However, Department E, which is part of the process, knows nothing about Department B or the problem; does not know much about Department A; but does know a lot about the way they work with C and D. Someone from each area must be

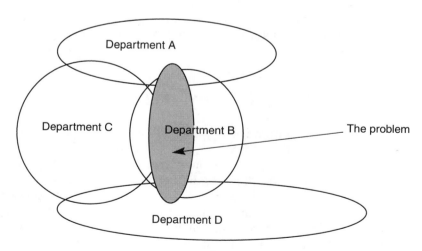

Fig 6.2 Who knows about the problem?

part of the team to solve the problem and to improve the process if the solution is to be workable, because any solution will effect C and D and therefore is likely to have some effect on E. To build a long-lasting solution requires the brain power of all of those involved in the process. A, B, C, D and E could also simply be functions, sections or individuals.

The team is thus formed objectively from a consideration of the process not the people. However, as more teams are formed it is important not to choose the same people all of the time, although a number of people with specialist skills will always be highly sought. It is important to include new people from sections to spread the involvement and the true empowerment as wide as possible. At times this will need a lot of firm resolve and trust together with a lot of care with less-forthcoming, new team members who will need coaching.

This method of developing an improvement team by studying those individuals who know, understand and who are involved in the process to be improved is similar to that used by the Japanese to establish their *kaizen* teams. They are said to make a slight change, in that the team leader sits down and starts to map the process under improvement. When the leader's knowledge of the process is exhausted, they invite another person from the area about which knowledge is lacking. This person completes the part of the map they know about and others join in the say way until the process map is complete and they are agreed that it is complete. Then they have the right team to improve the process.

It is usually good practice to set up some form of matrix to monitor the use of team resources. Such a matrix will have two functions: it will show if individuals are becoming involved in too many teams; and will show who is available to join or rejoin teams. If you are using a computer to manage the projects, this could be incorporated in the program using a simple spreadsheet; if not, a simple paper system will be sufficient. See Figure 6.3 as an example.

THE VALUE OF FACILITATORS

Maintaining early momentum is a topic we will consider from several different aspects during this book. At this point we need to consider resources. Within the senior management group, one individual will be nominated as the project co-ordinator, the TQ champion and facilitator to the senior team, as a team. Each member of the senior team will sponsor a key improvement project, often leading the team themselves and always taking full responsibility for the achievement of the performance improvement required. However, this is not enough in most organisations, even small ones. It has been found by a number of organisations to be worth the

Project names

Employee names

Fig 6.3 Team resource utilisation matrix

investment to appoint and to train others, from a complete cross-section of the organisation, to act as facilitators in their area.

Typically, an organisation should be looking in the first instance to nominate about one facilitator to every 30 employees. The facilitator's main attribute is a passion for quality. One role in the early stages will be to assist with the awareness programme, those who have the ability will assist with the actual delivery of the training. After that they will help set up the 'bottom up' teams, leading the initial meetings while they train the team leaders in the skills of holding effective meetings, following the systematic approach of the quality improvement cycle and using the TQ tools appropriately. As time passes, so the facilitator's role will become firm.

Responsibilities

The responsibilities of a facilitator are:

- to provide guidance and support to line management and staff in the activities of cultural change;
- to be the local TQ expert;
- to facilitate improvement teams;
- to identify and help to remove blockages and barriers to the change process;
- to be a motivator of teams and a solver of team problems;
- to act as help-line for individuals, team leaders, managers;
- to be a catalyst for change;
- to be a communicator and role model;
- to share best practice with other facilitators.

Activities

These include:

- provide training in meeting skills;
- running parts of the early meetings to establish the standard for effective meetings and teamwork;
- provide training and coaching in the use of TQ tools;
- give feedback on team performance;
- provide an external, wider perspective to the discussion;
- assist by acting as a relatively impersonal sounding board for team members;
- facilitate discussions to help the team discover its own answers;
- *listening*, not talking.

A facilitator is not ...

The role of the facilitator should not be confused with others'. A facilitator is not:

- the improvement team leader;
- doer of the project;
- subject matter expert for the project;
- management puppet;
- unavailable;
- dictatorial, dogmatic;
- biased, prejudiced, political;
- the best.

SUPPORT FOR IMPROVEMENT TEAMS

All improvement teams, 'top down' and 'bottom up' will rely on a sponsor who is task-oriented and who provides line management authority to implement recommended changes. There will also be a team of facilitators who will provide the necessary advice to ensure that the team's work is carried out thoroughly and effectively. Facilitators come from all areas of the business in addition to the specialists in the quality assurance team. The facilitator is process-oriented. Figure 6.4 (overleaf) provides a model for support of the facilitator.

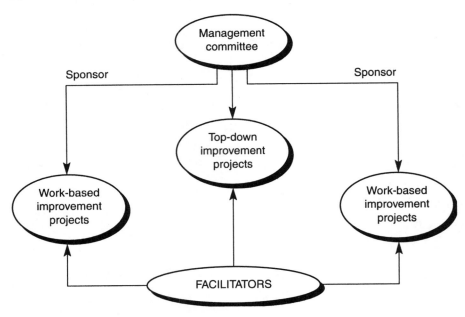

Fig 6.4 Sponsor/facilitator/support model

7

Developing a Measurement Culture

'A Team without a scoreboard is only practising'
Roger Milliken

- **The need for a measurement culture**
- **Natural work team structures**
- **Goal deployment to everyone**
- **Accountability – up, down and across the organisation**

INTRODUCTION

In chapter 2 we looked at the establishment of *key measures* for the organisation as a whole. Now we are going to consider the cascade of the *mission, core objectives* and *key performance improvement targets* into the organisation down the management line to the individual and the setting of individual performance targets, action plans and measures. Figure 7.1 shows the world class organisation model, with the focus on goal-driven measurement.

As we have said before, things don't just happen, management has to take visible action to make things happen. Developing a *measurement culture* is no exception. Managers must challenge their teams to say what they intend to do in order to make a difference in the shaping of the future and the achievement of the key performance targets.

To do this you have to plan carefully on three separate fronts:

- establish customer-focused, natural, work teams;
- identify which of the key performance measures each team can influence;
- arrange special meetings with each team to explain what is required and to facilitate the establishment of a team mission statement, goals, measures, improvement targets and action plans to achieve the improvement targets.

You may well have already considered the organisational structure and taken steps to reorganise through a focus on process. You may not want to take such a step yet, but to start to establish a measurement culture, you

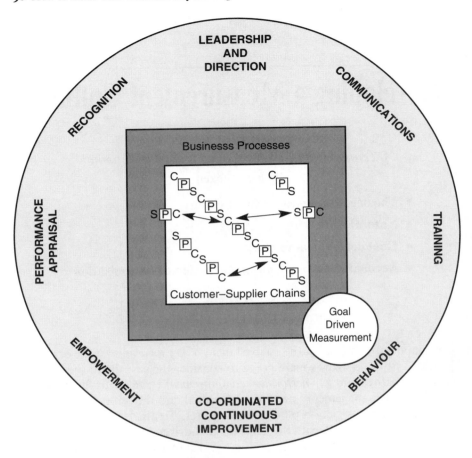

Fig 7.1 World class organisation model: measurement

will have to consider a team structure of some sort based on natural work groups or process groups. An example of this can be seen in Figure 7.2.

To determine who can influence what, it is useful to set up a matrix listing all of the employees of the organisation down one side and all of the key performance measures across the top. Grouping the employees in their teams is also helpful at this stage. With this matrix you are able to consider in the first instance, each team and then each individual, asking the question 'by what they do (team or individual), can they influence this performance measure?' Some of the measures can only be influenced by the top-down improvement teams or through the steering committee setting up further cross functional teams for the specific purpose.

Example 1: a manufacturing company

- Management committee
- Manufacturing teams comprising people carrying out the following functions:

  Production Control
  Planning
  Technical
  Quality Assurance
  Human Resources
  Operators
  No separate department other than for company-wide roles

- Sales and marketing teams
- Human resource development, planning and training team
- Finance team
- Technical, research and development team
- Logistics team

Example 2: a distribution company

- Customer service teams comprising people carrying out the following functions:

  Sales development
  Sales order
  Purchasing and inventory management
  Delivery
  Quality assurance

- Warehouse teams comprising:

  Warehouse operators
  Quality assurance
  Goods in
  Despatch

Fig 7.2 Examples of establishing natural work teams

There will be some measurements that are best collected by nominated individuals, who may not be able to directly influence them, but are best placed to report the effects as well as collecting the data. Such individuals should be identified within the matrix at this time.

Armed with this clear view of who can influence what and who should be responsible for data collection and reporting to the steering committee, you can arrange formal sessions with each team to communicate the need to establish responsibility for measurement and taking action to improve. By this activity alone you can make all the good words of the launch and the awareness training come alive to the employees (Figure 7.3).

The tool to use here to provide the teams with some focus is *team purpose* analysis. In chapter 5 we discussed the use of team purpose analysis to get things started in the team or section following the launch and the initial awareness training. Using it in the cascading responsibility for achieving the key performance targets provides a consistent vehicle to link the deployment of the mission and goals at the start, with team and individual performance improvement goals, together with the key measures of success through the *team purpose analysis* methodology (see chapter 15), which focuses on the output of each team and the requirements of its customers. An example is worked through schematically in Figure 7.4.

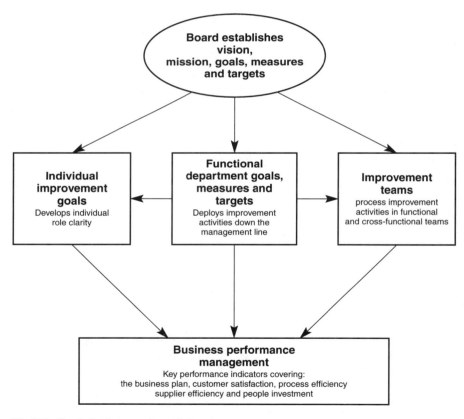

Fig 7.3 Goal deployment model

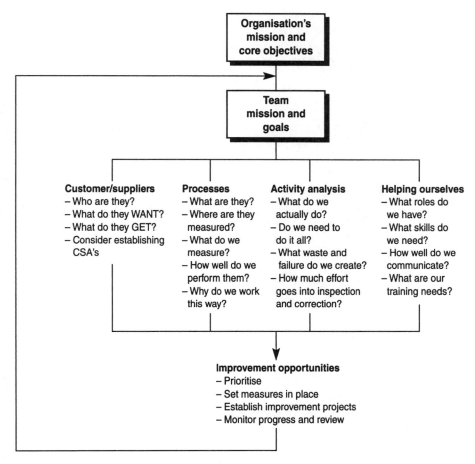

Fig 7.4 Team purpose analysis with mission and goals deployment

All of the outputs form the formal sessions with the teams and the outputs of the team purpose analysis should be documented as a reference for the improvement activity. Agreed follow-up sessions to review progress in the initial stages must be established, for although you are going to use the improvement activity to establish *empowerment* it still must be monitored and reviewed regularly.

There is a line of report and accountability and that is through the team leaders to the steering committee.

This activity, as with all activities within a total quality environment, should be approached from the view point of Deming's quality improvement cycle, *plan, do, check, act*. In this instance, careful preparation before involving the teams, followed by the briefing itself and the establishment of team performance targets. The follow-up and any subsequent corrective action to promote the permanent establishment of the *measurement culture* completes the cycle. It continues with regular review and future cascades as successive goal deployments take place.

Once the responsibility for measuring individual performance has been established through the deployment of the *key performance targets* it is a short step to individual measurement of all activity. The use of *customer supplier agreements* (see chapter 15) at both team and individual level is a further aid to encouraging the measurement culture and constructive feedback; measurement without fear.

Truly, as Rodger Milliken says, '... unless you measure what you are doing you are only practising.' it is only when everyone sees the need to measure key outputs in a way that prevents quality drift and encourages process improvement that you can say we have a measurement culture.

8

Leading and Managing Customer-Focused Teams

Creating a teamwork culture in which people really feel part of a team

- **Introducing teamwork**
- **What is a team?**
- **Why use them?**
- **John Adair's action-centred leadership model has a place in a total quality culture**
- **Assessing team performance**
- **Team behaviour checklist**
- **Effective meetings**
- **The team leader role**

INTRODUCTION TO USING TEAMS

The most powerful of the manageable elements in the establishment of a world class organisation is the management and empowerment of people in teams to solve problems and make improvements to processes. When first faced with the prospect of permitting the workforce to both make and take decisions affecting the way the organisation operates, most managers quake. Ideas of lost power, control, accountability and visions of chaos and anarchy abound. These visions could not be further from the truth. By unlocking the latent power that is within all individuals, a power born of their intimate knowledge of the problems and failures within their own processes, the result will provide the capability of achieving an organisation's full potential. That will require, closer, more skillful and innovative management than any traditional, autocratic situation.

In fact, managing people in teams is the easy part, creating a teamwork culture is much more difficult. There are many 'teams' at work in an organisation, some are more visible than others. People recognise the functional group as a team fairly easily, they have more difficulty with the 'process' team and the bigger the organisation the harder it is for people to equate to the organisational 'team' and their belonging to it.

If one studies world class organisations closely, one common theme they all have is a sense of *pride* in the organisational 'team' that can be found in everybody, at all levels.

The objective of this chapter is to demonstrate the key elements, skills and processes needed to manage people in teams to achieve effective data gathering. In turn, this leads to problem-solving and the continuous improvement of the organisation's processes and systems and most importantly a sense of belonging to a team.

Using these skills effectively, the team approach can be brought into effect rapidly, whilst maintaining the desired control over the rate of process and cultural change. It will give an understanding of the role of teams in roll out of the continuous improvement process.

This chapter provides the opportunity for readers to discover more about the way teams work and to understand the change that takes place within the team as the members move from independence to interdependence, and develop the trust in one another that is vital for a change in the culture of the organisation and real problem-solving and quality improvement. During this process, an understanding will develop regarding the particular role of the senior management sponsor, the team leader and the facilitator, and appreciate the powerful role of the individual. Forming, establishing, developing and leading teams is a fundamental management function. In normal operation there is time to move through some of the stages at a pace set by the teams, but when implementing a continuous improvement culture, there is a need for fast results and often the teams are not those that you would willingly form. These situations must be managed with adroitness and care to achieve the desired results.

What is a team?

Let us firstly consider the question, 'What is A Team?' A team consists of a number of elements:

- one *common* aim;
- a group of *individuals* with individual *skills* working *together*;
- common *goals*;
- *synergy*;

- a group with a *leader*;
- *consensus*.

In some part, all these characteristics can be achieved by many different types of group, but only a team will have all of them all of them all of the time. One single skill all team members must develop is that of *listening*.

Teamwork is achieving as a group more than could be achieved as individuals, by the pooling of skills, experience and expertise on the part of the members to achieve an agreed aim.

Why use teams ?

Teams and teamwork form one of the cornerstones of a world class organisation. Certainly it is the *interdependence* found in the teamwork of the Japanese business culture that makes it appear so formidable. A successful total quality culture can only be achieved by moving those people involved in the business from the mind set of individualism and independence, *where there is little sharing of ideas or information*, to the interdependence of teamwork which is the critical factor in the quest for continuing improvement and real problem solving.

Once interdependence has been achieved you will have created an environment where all resources are motivated to make continuous improvements. This will be marked by the natural development of a series of large and small informal teams. However, the strength of a world class culture lies not just with such informal teams but with the effective use of *two* types of formal team.

Quality improvement teams

A quality improvement team is a group of people with appropriate knowledge, skill and experience brought together by management to tackle and solve a particular problem, usually on a project basis. They are cross functional and multi-disciplined. They will take a broad view and work on an entire *process* (or operating system).

Quality circles

A quality circle (team) is a group of employees involved in associated work who meet *voluntarily* at frequent and regular intervals to discuss problems encountered in their work with a view to discovering solutions to these problems. The circles are installed with full *managerial support*. Quality circles do not deal with complete processes as a project. They have other aspects, *social*, *technical* and *educational*, as a part of their function. Quality circles require a leader, trained in the art of running meetings, to teach and supervise members so that they can all participate and thereby grow. In practice, these have no place in the implementation of TQM – other than as a formal structure within the communication process – until well into the programme.

Part of the management of this teamwork element is to provide leadership to both the *formal teams*, and in doing so create the environment for the *informal teams* to develop and flourish. It has to be recognised that this is a slow, gradual, process that is led from the top by the total commitment of the senior management team, who themselves must make a speedy transition from *independence* to *interdependence*, genuinely and openly, to give the signal and example to the rest of the employees through their demonstration of teamwork.

We mentioned in chapter 3 the British Airways experience which demonstrated how significant an effect senior management behaviour had on bringing about cultural change. Today's senior management behaviour is tomorrow's *company policy*; and in this case team working is *the way we **all** do things round here*.

Customers, both internal and external, know when you are not meeting their requirements, but they are not *delighted* when their requirements are met, they remain just neutral. However, if, as managers, you are to bring about the transformation that will ensure your organisation gets the full benefits from the team approach to problem-solving and continuous improvement you must understand what motivates people and how to manage and motivate teams.

ACTION-CENTRED LEADERSHIP

Although it was established many years ago, for a model of effective leadership and management of people in teams we need look no further than the concept of action-centred leadership developed by Dr John Adair. It certainly lives well in the fast-changing world of total quality management, and could have almost been created for it. During the 1960s Adair was senior lecturer in military history and the leadership training advisor at the Royal Military Academy, Sandhurst. Later, as assistant director of the Industrial Society, he developed what he called the action-centred leadership model, based on his real experience at Sandhurst. His responsibility there had been to ensure that results in cadet training did not fall below a certain standard. He observed that some instructors frequently achieved well-above average results due to their own natural ability with groups and their enthusiasm.

He used this experience to develop the model of a team approach which is the basis for our approach to the leadership of quality teams.

Over the years there has been much academic work (mostly in the US) on the psychology of teams, and on the leadership of teams (see chapter 4 on motivation). One thing they agree about is that teams develop a personality and culture of their own. They respond to leadership and motivation according to rules usually applied to individuals.

In developing his model, Adair related the main approaches of Maslow, Herzberg and McClelland to what he knew and had observed. In his model, Adair has brought it out, clearly, that for any group or team, big or small, to respond to leadership, they need a clearly defined *task*, and the response and achievement of that task is interrelated to the needs of the *team* and the separate needs of the *individual members* of the *team*. Figure 8.1 shows Adair's model of action-centred leadership.

The value of the overlapping circles in Figure 8.1 is to emphasise the unity of leadership and the interdependence of the three areas of the group. It is sufficient here to recognise that effective leaders are aware of the interdependence and multi-functional reaction to single decisions affecting any of the three areas. So this is where we start. Let us consider the needs of the individual components of the group model. Drawing upon the discipline of social psychology, Adair developed, and applied to training, the functional view of leadership. The essence of this he distilled into the three interrelated but distinctive requirements of a leader. These are: to define and achieve the job or task; to build up and co-ordinate a team to do this; and to develop and satisfy the individuals within the team.

- *Task needs* The difference between a team and a random crowd is that a team has some common purpose, goal or objective, e.g. a football team. If a work team doesn't achieve the required result or a meaningful result

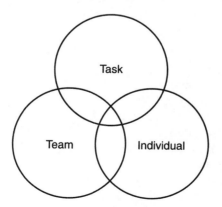

Fig 8.1 Adair's model of action-centred leadership

it will become frustrated. Organisations have a task: to make a profit, to provide a service, or even to survive. So anyone who manages others has to achieve results: production, marketing, selling or whatever. Achieving objectives is a major criterion of success.

- *Team needs* To achieve its objectives, the group needs to be held together. People need to be working in a co-ordinated fashion in the same direction and teamwork will ensure that the team's contribution is greater than the sum of its parts. Conflict within the team must be used effectively, arguments can generate ideas, or act destructively to breed tension and lack of co-operation.

- *Individual needs* Within working groups, individuals have their own set of needs. They need to know what their responsibilities are, how they will be needed, how well they're performing. They need an opportunity to show their potential, take on responsibility and receive recognition for good work.

I said earlier that this model could almost have been created for a total quality culture; most of the environmental elements of my world class model are here.

The team functions

In the same way as the elements of the team model have needs, the achievement of those needs requires a number of functions to be performed consistently (a process):

- *Task functions;*
  - defining the task;
  - making a plan;
  - allocating work and resources;
  - controlling quality and tempo of work;
  - checking performance against the plan;
  - adjusting the plan.

- *Group functions;*
  - setting standards;
  - maintaining discipline;
  - building team spirit;
  - encouraging, motivating, giving a sense of purpose;
  - appointing sub-leaders;
  - ensuring communication within the group;
  - training the group.
- *Individual functions;*
  - attending to personal problems;
  - praising individuals;

- giving status;
- recognising and using individual abilities;
- training the individual.

Let us now concentrate on the small central area in Figure 8.1 where all three overlap. This is the leaders task area, or facilitator's area of operation. In an organisation which is attempting to introduce a world class or TQ culture, this is the *action for change* area, where you are attempting to manage the change from *business as usual* through the overlaying of *world class culture* to the point where:

WORLD CLASS = BUSINESS AS USUAL

This is achieved by using the cross-functional quality improved teams as the strategic interface.

In the action area the team leader's (facilitator's) task is similar to the task outlined by John Adair. The leader must try to satisfy all three areas of need by achieving the task, building the team and satisfying individual needs. The leader who concentrates only on the task, for example, in going all out for production schedules while neglecting the training, encouragement and motivation of the team and individuals, may do well in the short term. Eventually, however, those people will give less effort than they are capable.

Similarly, a leader who concentrates only on creating team spirit while neglecting the task and the individuals will not get a maximum contribution from the team. They may enjoy working in a happy fashion in the team, but will lack the real sense of achievement which comes from accomplishing a task to the utmost of individual ability.

So the leader/facilitator must try to achieve a balance by acting in all three areas of overlapping need. It is always wise to work out a list of required leadership functions within the context of any given situation, but based on a general agreement as to the essentials. Here is Adair's original Sandhurst list on which you might base your own adaptation:

- *Planning*: e.g. seeking all available information.
  - Defining group task, purpose or goal.
  - Making a workable plan (in right decision-making framework).

- *Initiating*: e.g. briefing group on the aims and the plan.
  - Explaining why aim or plan is necessary.
  - Allocating tasks to group members.
  - Setting group standards.
- *Controlling*: e.g. maintaining group standards.
  - Influencing tempo.
  - Ensuring all actions are taken towards objectives.

    – Keeping discussion relevant.
    – Prodding group to action/decision.

- *Supporting*: e.g. expressing acceptance of persons and their contribution.
  - Encouraging group and individuals.
  - Disciplining group and individuals.
  - Creating team spirit.
  - Relieving tension with humour.
  - Reconciling disagreements or getting others to explore them.

- *Informing*: e.g. clarifying task and plan.
  - Giving new information to the group, i.e. keeping them 'in the picture'.
  - Receiving information from group.
  - Summarising suggestions and ideas coherently.

- *Evaluating*: e.g. checking feasibility of an idea.
  - Testing the consequences of a proposed solution.
  - Evaluating group performance.
  - Helping the group to evaluate its own performance against standards.

Let us now turn attention to those three overlapping areas. The facilitator has a role to manage these, particularly. If we move the three circles apart a little, as in Figure 8.2, we can focus on the overlap areas.

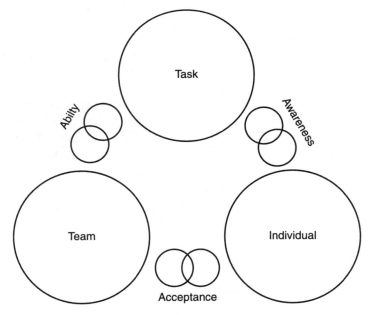

Fig 8.2 Facilitator's areas of responsibility

Task – team interface

The attention and responsibility of the facilitator is very much the selection of the individuals comprising the group, internal leadership, group dynamics, their individual and group skill levels, do they collectively as a *team* have the ability to achieve the *task* (or *solve the problem*). Additional information, training, support in terms of finding somewhere to meet, secretarial support, skill in running meetings for the leader, all will affect the ability of the team to succeed. So let us label that interface as *ability*.

Task – individual interface

Having chosen the right *individuals* for a balanced team, what is their understanding of the *task*? How well has the problem been explained? What is their level of understanding of the continuous improvement programme? Do they appreciate why they were chosen, what their role is and what the ultimate culture and mind set changes are? The success of this interface can be summed up as *awareness*.

Individual – team or team–individual interface

Are there any hidden agendas between *individuals* within the *team*? Does the leader permit participation within the group? Does the individual accept their role within the group? These are three issues to be addressed, as is acceptance of the team as an entity by the rest of the organisation. The acceptance of their role within the *team* by the *individual* and the importance of that role, openness and free exchange of ideas is the key to this interface. So we will label it *acceptance*.

We have now investigated the four overlapping areas in the Adair model in terms of the implementation and the continuous improvement process of TQM using teams. To help you to ensure you have taken account of all the team requirements as leader or facilitator, Figure 8.3 provides a checklist:

In dealing with the group as an individual or any individual of the group, a *situational style* of leadership must be adopted (chapter 4). These groups (teams) and the individuals within them will to some extent be starting cold, but they will develop and grow in both strength and experience. The interface between the external leader (facilitator) must also change with the change in the group. Initially adopting a very *directive approach*, giving clear instructions to meet agreed goals.

Facilitating to a high level of involvement initially helping with all aspects of the quality improvement team operation. Gradually, as they learn, become more experienced and have some success, you will move

Task
1. Are the *targets* clearly set out? ☐
2. Are there clear *standards of performance*? ☐
3. Are available *resources* defined? ☐
4. Are responsibilities clear? ☐
5. Are *available resources* fully utilised? ☐
6. Are *targets* and *standards* being defined? ☐
7. Is a *systematic* approach being used? ☐

Team
1. Is there a *common* sense of *purpose*? ☐
2. Is there a *supportive* climate? ☐
3. Is the unit (team) *growing* and *developing*? ☐
4. Is there a sense of corporate *achievement*? ☐
5. Is there a sense of *common identity*? ☐
6. Does the team know and respond to the leader's *vision*? ☐

Individual
1. Is each individual *accepted* by the, leader and the team? ☐
2. Is each individual *involved* by the, leader? ☐
3. Is each individual able to *contribute*? ☐
4. Does each individual know what is *expected* in relation to the *task* and the *team*? ☐
5. Does each individual *feel part* of a team? ☐
6. Is there evidence of individual *growth*? ☐

Fig 8.3 Team–task individual checklist

through coaching and support to less directing and eventually a less supporting and less directive approach. This will happen more as an interdependent style permeates the whole organisation.

THE BENEFITS OF USING TEAMS

Even the most simple problems at the outset are in fact quite complex when you attempt to find the root cause to eliminate them rather than going for a quick fix. For this reason alone, using teams gives you the benefit of *pooling expertise* and *resources* and focusing it at one time on the problem. By assembling a team to tackle a problem you are being time efficient because it is much more time-consuming to have a series of one-to-one contacts whilst trying it solve a problem.

In finding the solution to any problem, there is a potential for conflict, particularly with those who must implement the solution. By assembling a team which understands the process and the problem, all actual and potential areas of conflict can be dealt with as the team finds the root cause and builds a solution together.

People look at problems from their own perspective with a mixture of experience and personal preference. Each therefore brings a specific input to the decision-making. A good team that is well-led and resourced, which works together as a team will make very good decisions, of a much higher order than those made by individuals struggling with a problem and a decision on their own. In poor teams the level of decision-making can be a lot worse than the individual.

Once a decision has been made on a solution to a problem, the participation in building the solution cements ownership. This leads to improved implementation of change as the team own the outcome and are committed to making it work. The team environment provides a situation where people find they can grow and as individuals grow within an organisation, so the organisation can grow too.

The team process

The operation of a team is a process, it has inputs and outputs and the process itself is a function of the leadership style, the motivation of the individuals as a result of that leadership and the interaction of the group. It is this interaction within the team, which gives each team its unique character that we call *team dynamics*.

All teams undergo a number of changes as they develop. The initial stages are crucial in establishing a good working group and the facilitator or team leader must be very watchful during this period.

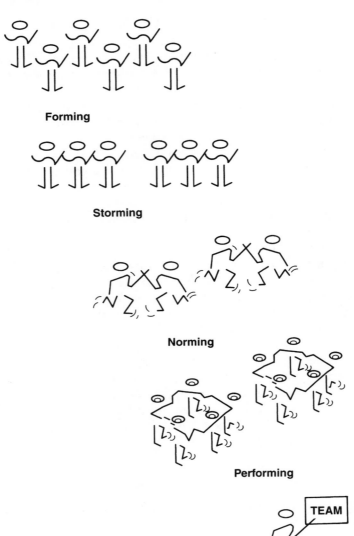

Forming

Storming

Norming

Performing

TEAM

Fig 8.4 Stages in team development

Stages in team development

Teams go through four development stages and a possible fifth stage when their task is completed. The stages, which are summarised in Figure 8.4, are known as forming, storming, norming and performing.

Forming   is the initial stage when the team is brought together for the first time. The general characteristics of this stage are people being very formal with each other, the leader and facilitator. Feelings, weakness, and mistakes are kept hidden. There is little care shown for each other's views, and there is no shared understanding of what needs to be done. If the group shows no signs of moving on to the *storming* stage, look out for individuals confining themselves to their defined jobs, increasing tendency to produce paperwork and to be bureaucratic and the leader being over-firm and traditional.

Storming   is the second stage and may be reached more quickly, especially if the team members have some experience of the process. The stage is reached when team members want to face the problems more openly, (looking for prevention rather than detection and looking for improvement not punishment).

During the *storming* stage, more risky personal issues are opened up and the group becomes more inward-looking and members start to listen to one another's views. However, do not mistake any apparent openness for *trust*. Only issues that will show the individual in a good light will be opened. Team members are manoeuvring for position within the team. The team still lacks the capacity to act in a unified, economic and effective way. There is a danger during this stage that individuals will become too focused on negative and personal issues and their own agenda may be created. They need to pass through this stage, not get trapped by it.

Norming   once the team gets through the storming stage, members begin to have confidence in each other and the *trust* to look at how the team itself is operating. The team adopts a more systematic, open, approach which leads to a more methodical way of working. Decisions are made by:

- clarifying the purpose;
- establishing objectives;
- collecting information and facts;
- considering options;
- detailing plans;
- reviewing to improve.

Performing   having established a basis of trust during the norming stage, there is now a basis for a really *mature team*, where:

- flexibility and interdependence are the keynotes;
- leadership is decided by situations, not by protocol;
- everyone's energies are used for the team;
- the team considers basic principles and social aspects of the organisation's decisions.

Mourning   in the early stages of introducing teamwork, and particularly after a long, high profile project, you may detect an air of mourning when a team disbands. This can effect work adversely and more errors and mistakes may be made. This can be headed off by allowing a small continuing role in monitoring the effect of the improvement.

Assessing team performance

An important role of the manager or supervisor as facilitator is the assessment of team performance in order to provide effective coaching. The facilitator should be looking for :

- how leadership is exercised;
- how decision-making is accomplished;
- how team resources are used;
- how new members are integrated into the team.

Effective working teams which are performing, typically have:

- *clear objectives and agreed goals* identifying common tasks, working within agreed guide lines;
- *openness and confrontation* listening to each other but being open and frank, not hiding things, and challenging each other;
- *support and trust* communicating with each other, accepting criticism and guidance;
- *co-operation and conflict* acting on suggestions but arguing good cases;
- *good decision-making* ensuring all members contribute to the solution;
- *appropriate leadership* allowing the leadership to pass around the group depending on expertise, using the specialists in the team but ensuring that the leader retains overall control;
- *review of team process* consulting within the group and looking for opportunities to improve the team process;

- *individual development opportunities* helping individuals to apply their skills and learn from others in order to maximise their potential.
- *fun* using humour within the group even when the going gets tough. Team experiences should be *fun* and it tends to spill over into the workplace.

Attributes of high performance teams can be seen in terms of the Adair model as having:

- *high* levels of *task* fulfilment;
- *high* levels of *team* maintenance;
- *low* levels of *self*-orientation.

Facilitators and teams themselves need to monitor and measure their performance regularly using a checklist, recording the results and analysing the trends, and taking action to improve.

In assessing *task fulfilment* you will be looking for:

- *Initiating* actively putting forward ideas, finding solutions, defining problems, suggesting procedures and proposing task or goals;
- *Testing for consensus* checking readiness for decision-making, checking agreements;
- *Information-seeking – and giving* providing facts and opinions, suggestions and ideas;
- *Clarifying* analysing implications of information or ideas, interpreting, defining terms, indicating alternatives;
- *Summarising* reviewing progress, drawing together ideas and information.

A key function for the facilitator is team maintenance which requires:

- *encouraging* supporting contributions, stimulating contributions, being friendly and responsive;
- *setting standards* suggesting standards for group working arrangements, reviewing regularly against theses, evaluating reasons for group success as well as failure;
- *expressing group feelings* observing, understanding and expressing group emotions, reducing tension, mediating, recognising conflicts and encouraging exploration of differences. Finding and encouraging laughter also;
- *compromising* giving weight to others views, commitment to best solution;
- *gatekeeping* keeping communications and options open, facilitating participation, suggesting procedures for sharing discussion.

As the trust and understanding of interdependence takes over from independence, the level of *self-orientation* will be seen to fall. Behaviour to watch out for includes:

- *Blocking* interpose a difficulty without an option or without reason;
- *aggressiveness* attacking, over-painting the picture to stir up feelings, exaggeration;
- *dominating* asserting authority or superiority in manipulating the group, refusing to budge;
- *forming cliques* forming sub-groups within the team for protection or support;
- *Special pleading* speaking for special interests as a cover for personal interest;
- *Seeking sympathy* drawing attention, attempting to gain sympathy;
- *Withdrawing* opting out of the discussion or hiding behind stronger members' opinions;
- *wasting time* various diversionary tactics for self-oriented reasons;
- *not listening* pardon?

The team behaviour check list shown in Figure 8.5 should be copied and used regularly by various members of the team and individual observers from other teams. As members become more skilled at the team process, the number of instances of self-orientation will fall and scores for the other two areas will steadily increase for each member.

In the early stages with a highly committed group, high scoring will be seen in the task fulfilment category and in self-orientation but low in team maintenance. Keep a record of scores and trends.

RUNNING EFFECTIVE MEETINGS

The importance of effective meetings skills has already been discussed in chapter 4, but when teams meet it is important that meetings are run well. To run and lead an effective meeting, the team leader must take time to prepare well and it is the responsibility of managers to allow team leaders the necessary time to do this, however difficult. If the continuous improvement groups are to be effective, meetings must be productive, motivating and inspirational. Problems will not be solved by endless meetings. The objective of the team meeting is to share information, devise strategy, make decisions and plan assignments. It is the willing and timely completion of assignments by team members that will gather the information required to find the root cause and permit its elimination.

Team member					
Task fulfilment					
Initiating					
Information-seeking					
Clarifying					
Summarising					
Testing for consensus					
Team maintenance					
Encouraging					
Setting standards					
Expressing group feelings					
Harmonising					
Compromising					
Gatekeeping					
Self-orientation					
Blocking					
Aggressiveness					
Dominating					
Forming cliques					
Special pleading					
Seeking sympathy					
Withdrawing					
Wasting time					
Not listening					

Fig 8.5 Team behaviour checklist

To aid the process, meetings must be given recognition as important by providing a worthy place for it, defining a *start* and *finish* time to which everyone, including senior management members adheres. Finishing on time is also crucial to success as most members will be away from their work and will have had to arrange cover. An agenda which provides all information including the topics for discussion should be sent out well in advance; it will also help to keep the meeting on time. The agenda should provide a list of who should attend and any preparation required from each member, together with any supporting material. Never expect people to read newly-introduced material or reports during the meeting; it is a waste of time and many will require time to consider and prepare a response.

The team should appoint a 'secretary' to prepare and issue minutes, not just as a record of what took place but as a reminder to everyone of what it was they agreed to do before the next meeting. It removes doubt and misunderstanding. For this reason, minutes should be issued quickly after each meeting. This will add to the formal nature of the meetings and the teams and show that they are not a game.

The role of the team leader

In addition to preparing well for each of the meetings, it is the role of the leader to make contact with every team member regularly to ensure they have no problems. Any problems that cannot be resolved by the team leader should be referred to the facilitator or sponsor.

In the meetings, the leaders share ideas and opinions and encourage other points of view. They should listen 'openly' and help the team arrive at the best solution possible – for the team, not the leader. Whilst leaders must reserve their judgement and not unduly influence teams, they must accept responsibility and support teams outside their sphere of operations.

It is important for the leader to create a 'climate' for creativity and encourage contributions from all: to help different views to emerge and remove barriers to idea generation by supporting creativity.

It is worth remembering that most of the problems being dealt with by the teams have never been solved properly before, that is eliminated permanently by locating the root cause. In the past, solutions have been no more than a papering over of the cracks time and time again. New ideas and radical solutions are often needed.

It is often worth testing your ability as a team leader by asking individual members of the team to carry out a review of the meeting. You carry out a review too and compare your rating with the ratings of the other members. A team meeting review checklist is given as Figure 8.6.

	10 5 0	
1. Goal clear and agreed	⊔⊔⊔⊔⊔⊔⊔⊔⊔⊔	Goal unclear
2. Previous agreements complete	⊔⊔⊔⊔⊔⊔⊔⊔⊔⊔	Partially or not at all
3. We listened to each other	⊔⊔⊔⊔⊔⊔⊔⊔⊔⊔	No awareness of listening
4. Right people present	⊔⊔⊔⊔⊔⊔⊔⊔⊔⊔	Team not correctly composed
5. Leadership needs creatively met	⊔⊔⊔⊔⊔⊔⊔⊔⊔⊔	Drifting or dominating
6. Open trusting atmosphere	⊔⊔⊔⊔⊔⊔⊔⊔⊔⊔	Distrust and defensiveness
7. Time used efficiently	⊔⊔⊔⊔⊔⊔⊔⊔⊔⊔	Time wasted
8. Systematic tools used	⊔⊔⊔⊔⊔⊔⊔⊔⊔⊔	Lack of systematric approach
9. Agreements reached (what/ who/when) and documented	⊔⊔⊔⊔⊔⊔⊔⊔⊔⊔	Verbal agreements or none
10. Consensus decisions	⊔⊔⊔⊔⊔⊔⊔⊔⊔⊔	Authoritarian or other
11. I was able to express my opinion	⊔⊔⊔⊔⊔⊔⊔⊔⊔⊔	No opportunity
12. Opinions could be questioned	⊔⊔⊔⊔⊔⊔⊔⊔⊔⊔	Opinions untouchable
13. Opinions distinguished from facts	⊔⊔⊔⊔⊔⊔⊔⊔⊔⊔	Mixed and not aware of it
14. Everyone involved	⊔⊔⊔⊔⊔⊔⊔⊔⊔⊔	Some not involved
15. Challenging rewarding committed atmosphere	⊔⊔⊔⊔⊔⊔⊔⊔⊔⊔	Flat and lifeless

Key

Unacceptable	0
Must be improved	1,2,3
Fair	4,5,6
Good	7,8,9
Excellent	10

Fig 8.6 Checklist for effective meetings

VALUING THE CONTRIBUTION OF EVERY INDIVIDUAL

Successful teamwork and meetings depend to a large extent on individuals being able to contribute, knowing that their contributions are valued and will make a difference. This is dependent on people and their views being respected. There is here, as it would seem everywhere in a world class culture, an interdependence between how we interact with each other. To maximise the effectiveness of this interaction, it is best to turn to the psychology of personal preferences, and take a look at the way in which people operate. Examples include the way people: focus their energy; gather information; make decisions; the general way they are; the way they respond to team challenges; interact with other members of the team and the unique way they contribute.

The best way of doing all of these things in a non-threatening way is to use the psychometric profiling device called Myers Briggs Type Indicator. It is an extremely rigorous way of looking into personality type and preference and the non-threatening way it is used, in not connecting any particular type with any particular job, makes it extremely useful in creating the teamwork environment. It helps better understanding of each other, opening the way to valuing differences between individuals and their contributions and assisting with a better understanding of ourselves. By understanding oneself and having an insight into other team members the team will be more effective and the use of Myers Briggs Type Indicator in this situation can identify areas of strength and weakness within the team; reduce unproductive work by building on individual strengths, clarify team behaviour; help to match specific task assignments to team members' preferred mode of operation; supply a framework within which members can control and understand conflict; help individuals understand how different perspectives and methods can aid problem-solving, and maximise a team's diversity in order to reach more useful and insightful conclusions.

Understanding not just that there is a difference in the way other people see a problem, the same problem, speeds up the improvement process and the establishment of trust within really effective working teams.

9

Establishing a Continuous Improvement Culture

Always asking '... is there a better way?'

- **Empowerment = learning to let go**
- **Top down and bottom up: two routes to improved performance**
- **The quality improvement cycle**
- **Paradigms: the barriers to real change**
- **Three approaches to continuous improvement**

INTRODUCTION

Getting people to support the initial thrust of cultural change and the early improvement teams is relatively easy, maintaining the momentum and establishing a *continuous improvement culture* is more difficult and must be managed, just as all the other elements of a world class culture must be managed. This management must be carried out in a variety of ways, ensuring that all ideas for improvement are captured and actioned, monitoring that there is time made available to work on the team tasks and controlling the use of resources in terms of the team members. Typically, there will be a tendency for particular individuals to be in high demand by different teams because of their willingness to get involved, to make things happen or their expertise.

The first improvement teams to be established are based on the 'top down' teams. They have very clear improvement objectives and typically lots of problems, both large and small, to work on. The resulting delegation to deal with each problem helps to spread the teamwork approach.

Once the awareness training has been completed there will be a flood of ideas for improvement from the rest of the workforce; these will require the establishment of a simple system for recording and monitoring action. These 'bottom up' ideas must be dealt with in one of four positive ways;

- recognition of the idea and a simple 'yes', get on with it yourself, i.e. *empowerment* to make it happen;

- recognition of the idea and a simple 'no', not for the moment, but it will be held in mind until other things more appropriate to the current business goals have been completed;
- recognition of the idea and 'yes' we will take it on board, it will need a team approach and we want you to establish a team, we will help you;
- recognition of the idea and 'yes' we will take it on board, it will need a team approach and there is a team already established into whose area of remit this falls and we want you to join that team to help make it happen.

Figure 9.1 demonstrates the type of team structure and shows the resulting cascade effect.

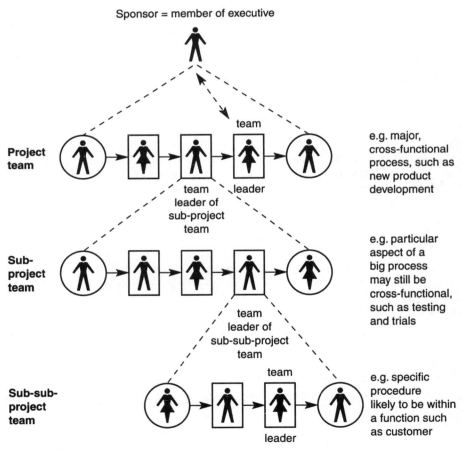

Fig 9.1 Project team cascade

A culture of continuous improvement requires control, and that control needs to be integrated with any systems which may already exist, such as 'corrective action' processes within a quality management system, customer complaints' procedures and suggestion schemes. Wherever possible, you must try to establish a single system to manage and control all of the improvements that result from each of these activities. An example of the basics of just such a system is shown in Figure 9.2 (overleaf).

Once the activity to improve a process has been set in motion from whatever quarter, a single methodology should be followed. Dr Deming, as we have already seen, suggested that only by continuously improving what we do and the way that we do it, can we hope to continue delighting our customers and ensuring that they keep on returning. In doing so he also suggested that it required a systematic approach which he called the 'quality improvement cycle' shown in Figure 9.3 (on page 125). He went on to suggest that by following his systematic approach the right sort of improvements would accrue at the appropriate times.

Quality improvement is more than just problem-solving, putting things right when they have gone wrong. To be successful, quality improvement must be a disciplined, continual activity. The quality improvement cycle with four simple stages – plan, do, check, act – helps to provide a framework for structured, systematic and disciplined approach to the solving of quality problems and implementing lasting solutions and improvements.

- PLAN   establish the facts:
          identify root causes;
          develop solutions(s);
          prepare plan to implement the solution.
- DO   implement the solution.
- CHECK   monitor progress against plan.
- ACT   make successful solutions permanent.

Good, effective planning is vital to the provision of customer satisfaction, the prevention of mistakes, errors and waste, and to the continuous improvement of what we do and the way we do it. But is this what we do? Perhaps our normal approach is more accurately described in Figure 9.4 (on page 125).

In an organisation that has not yet started out on the journey to becoming world class, as problems occur they tend to say:

- *What shall we do?* Insufficient effort is put into:
  - identifying and agreeing what the customer wants;
  - ensuring that the process is capable of delivering what the customer wants.
- *Do* Emphasis on action, must be doing something.

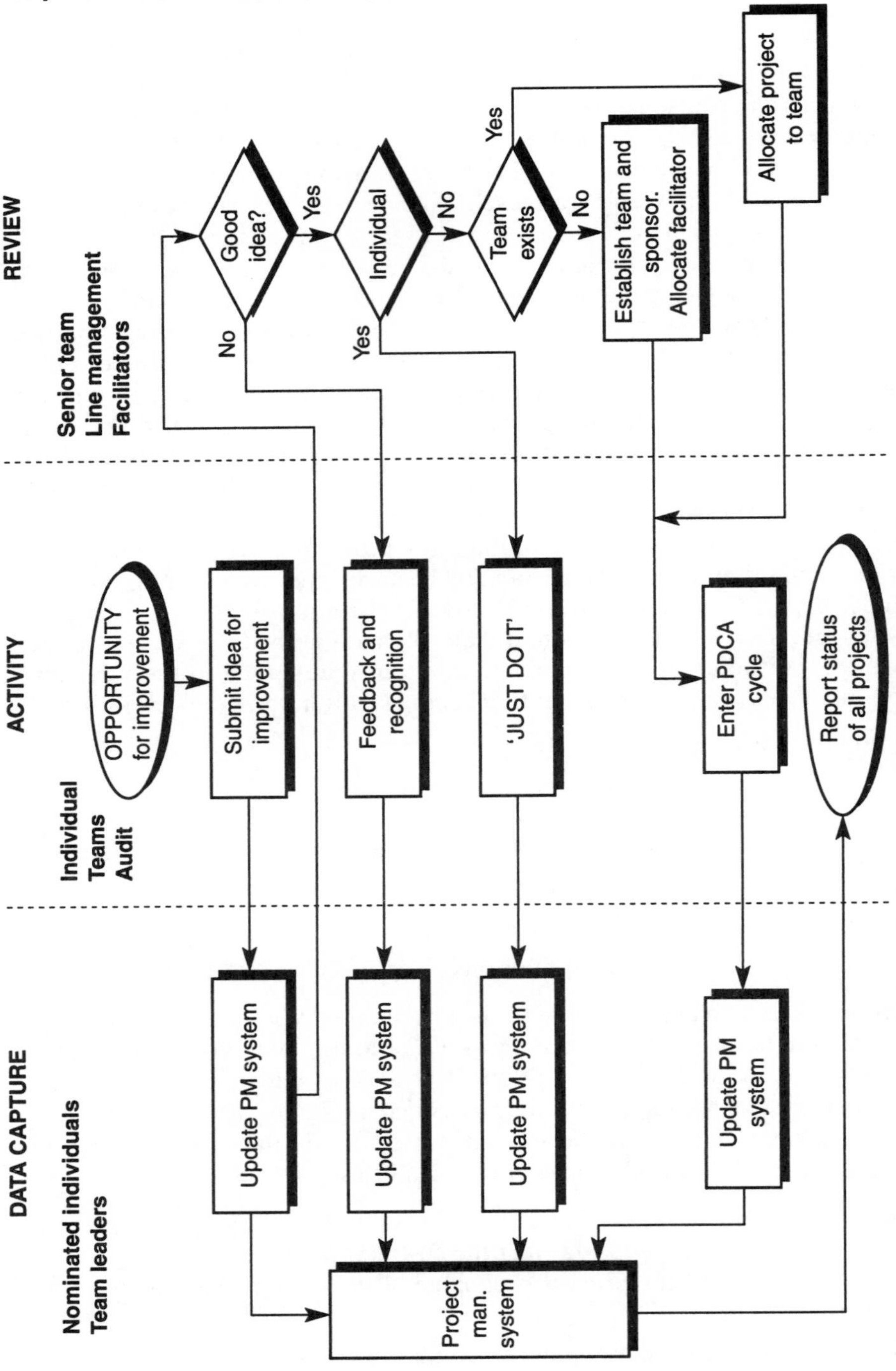

Fig 9.2 Outline of project management system. Capturing opportunities for improvement

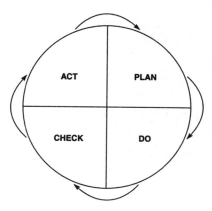

Fig 9.3 Deming's quality improvement cycle

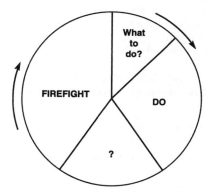

Do not allow your organisation to continue to work in this cycle:

What to do?: Insufficient effort put into:
• identifying and agreeing what the customer wants
• ensuring that the process is capable of delivering what the customer wants

Do: Emphasis is on action, must be doing something

Limited checks: Not enough effort put into checking whether the customer is satisfied with your output

Firefight: The result is lots of firefighting, wasted effort, and dissatisfied customers

Fig 9.4 How not to do it

- *Limited checks* Not enough effort put into checking whether the customer is satisfied with the output.
- *Firefight* The result is lots of firefighting, wasted effort and resources, and dissatisfied customers.

THE QUALITY IMPROVEMENT CYCLE

Figure 9.5 shows the stages of the cycle given in more detail.

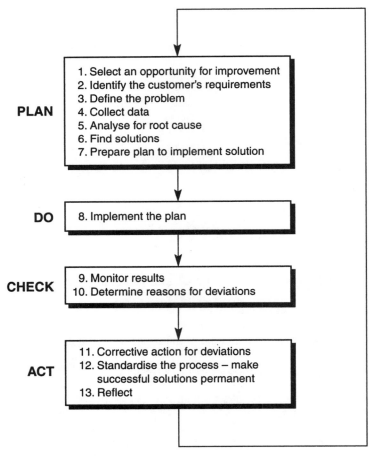

Fig 9.5 The quality improvement cycle

Plan

- *Select an opportunity for improvement:*
  - before selection, make sure all the possible options are identified;
  - generate a list of opportunities for improvement;
  - prioritise and select an opportunity.
- *Identify the customer's requirements:*
  - specify the customer by name;
  - know and analyse the customer requirements;
  - be prepared to help the customer to define the requirements precisely;
  - develop a customer–supplier agreement.
- *Define the problem:*
  - How do the customer's requirements compare with the current situation?
  - Define the problem to be solved.
- *Collect data:*
  - define and map the current process;
  - select measurements needed: before, during and after the process;
  - collect data for analysis.
- *Analyse for root causes:*
  - identify probable causes;
  - select the most probable causes and test if the root cause has been found;
  - define the root cause(s) of the problem.
- *Find solutions:*
  - develop criteria for solutions;
  - identify 'musts' versus 'wants';
  - generate possible solutions, evaluate against the wants and musts and select the best available solution;
  - Do *cost–benefit analysis*.
- *Prepare plan to implement solution:*
  - determine the expected improvement, set goals for improvement;
  - prepare initial action plan;
  - identify driving and restraining forces, prepare *force field analysis*;
  - finalise and agree the plan;
  - build in check points to monitor progress;
  - gain support from the key players, gain approval to implement the solution.

Do

- *Implement the plan:*
  - carry out the plan, implement the solutions.

Check

- *Monitor results – evaluate against plan:*
  - measure success against the customer's requirements and viewpoint;
  - is the customer delighted?
  - what benefits can be measured?
  - monitor implementation against check points – do not leave until implementation is complete.
- *Determine reasons for deviations:*
  - *where was the plan not successful?*
  - *ask why (five times)?*

Act

- *Corrective action for deviations:*
  - based on an understanding of why the plan was not successful, develop a new plan.
- *Standardise the process:*
  - make sure the gains that have been acheived are made permanent. (This is stabilising the improved process.)
- *Reflect:*
  - what have we learned? What's our start point for further improvement?

Notice the number of steps in the *plan* part of the cycle compared with the *do*, *check* and *act* parts of the cycle.
Remember it is:

Ready Aim Fire! not Ready Fire Aim!

But also beware of:

Ready Aim Aim Aim ... Aim!

The *quality improvement cycle* helps solve problems and identify and implement solutions in a disciplined way. When all managers and staff use the same process, teamwork can be significantly enhanced. At the end of chapter 8, reference was made to our psychological preferences. Left to our own preferred routes to solving problems and deciding on solutions, we all can take different paths with different outcomes.

MAKING CONTINUOUS PROCESS IMPROVEMENT

There are three separate, but to some extent interdependent, ways to improve the processes of the organisation. Process improvements can be brought about by:

- *breakthrough thinking* the big step changes in methods and thinking;
- *process stabilisation* bringing processes which are inherently variable under control or standardising a breakthrough, the benefits of which would otherwise slip away;
- *incremental improvement* continuous, small, step-by-step improvements – sometimes sponsored by benchmarking.

World class companies do all three of these all of the time. But why? The answer lies in trying to bridge the gap shown in Figure 9.6.

Whilst we are working away at gradual improvements, so are our competitors, they do not play fair in this particular battle. We must find new ways and step changes in what we do in order to catch up and overtake the competition.

Breakthrough thinking is aimed at introducing new ways and new processes. To do this involves setting stretching goals and usually results in producing incredible improvement and potentially improved capability through being creative and operating the process in a completely different way adding more value at the same time.

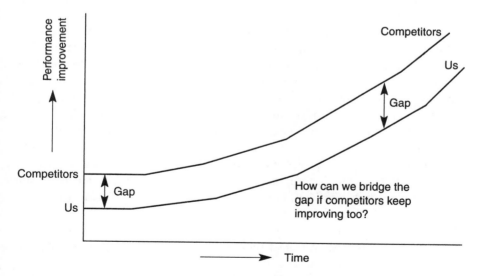

Fig 9.6 Graph of our improvement against competitors

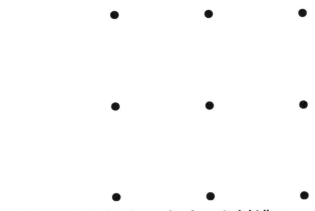

Fig 9.7 Connect all nine dots using four straight lines

Unfortunately, breakthrough thinking is not common, our minds are influenced by our *paradigms* or mind sets which limit our ability to see the possibilities presented by any given situation. People's thinking is conditioned considerably by these mind set constraints. To illustrate this, take a pencil and using *four* straight lines connect all nine dots in Figure 9.7, *without* taking the pencil from the paper. For the answer turn to the end of this chapter.

Your attempt was conditioned by your *paradigm* or mind set on connecting dots.

If you are going to make successful breakthroughs, moving the organisation on in quantum steps, you must *get outside your nine dots*. There are so many examples of breakthrough thinking in the world around us where people have managed to conceive ideas outside the traditional mind sets and see them through to implementation. Such ideas as microwave ovens (roasting a large turkey in a couple of hours, or baking a sponge cake in minutes, thought of as impossible at the time); photography without chemicals and water; the dry copier, an idea turned down by one photographic concern when shown to them – but where would we be without the photocopier today? And there are many others. New ideas should be investigated thoroughly, not dismissed out of hand just because they do not meet our paradigms. This may not be a comfortable approach for managers, but it is the only way to ensure breakthrough improvements are not missed.

However, in the initial stages you are not in control of new processes developed in this way, you must regain control of the new process, make it stable and predictable again if you are to continue to reap the initial benefits.

If you rely on breakthrough thinking alone, new advances will quickly slip back into old ways and sometimes to worse situations than before (Figure 9.8). You will need to know its new capability and how it will stand up to changes by customers. This action will eliminate firefighting and crisis management, both of which go hand in hand with 'not being in control' – the non-quality way. This is known as *process stabilisation*.

Process stabilisation can also be used to great effect on its own to improve erratic and inconsistent processes. It will involve the careful collection and analysis of key data about the process's characteristics. A study of the actual degree of variation and its nature. This process is called statistical process control, understanding how precisely the outputs of the process can be predicted and how much variation can be permitted before the process produces products or services which don't meet the specification. This book does not set out to provide detailed instruction on carrying out what is a very specialised task, suffice to say that having control of processes, understanding how consistent and robust a process is, is vital to providing confidence to everyone involved with it, customers, manager and operators. As has already been emphasised, it is a vital early step in benchmarking (chapter 15) to understand your process and to know that it is stable (little variation) and it produces what you expect (you are in control).

Process stabilisation of breakthrough improvements is not real improvement in itself, but it helps sustain the benefits from *breakthroughs*. So if we add the two together, breakthrough and stabilising, we develop the improvement model to become Figure 9.9 (overleaf).

There is a danger however that too much reliance on breakthrough and stabilising techniques will block access to the real wealth of experience and knowledge of the bulk of your people. You must also use the step-by-step approach to provide *incremental improvement* of the processes, through continuous improvement teams. Using small steps to continuously improve the capability of existing processes in order to optimise their performance –

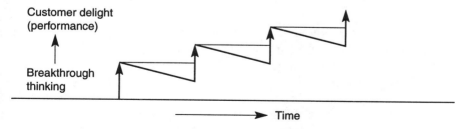

Fig 9.8 First stage of improvement model: breakthrough thinking alone allows things to slip back

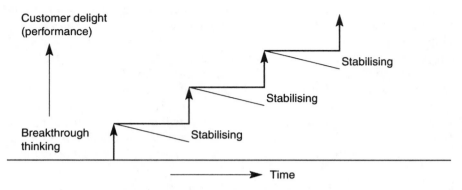

Fig 9.9 Second stage of improvement model: breakthrough thinking and stabilising

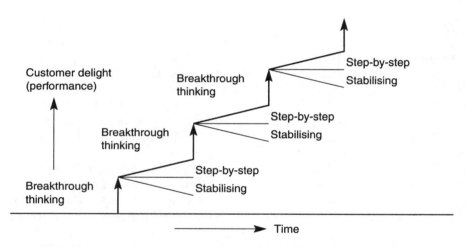

Fig 9.10 Third stage of improvement model: breakthrough thinking plus sta-bilising, plus step-by-step improvement

kaizen. This requires low investment in prevention through the involvement of all employees using the simple tools of total quality.

If we add all of these together then we get real process improvement, shown in Figure 9.10.

In all these situations, and especially to provide the regular incremental improvements, you need to apply the systematic approach provided by Deming's quality improvement cycle. It is often said by organisations that their teams have run out of ideas, or they have solved all the problems in their processes and cannot make any more improvement. What they are really saying is that they do not understand the cycle well enough. Regular review and challenge is needed, setting SMART goals that will stretch them – and practice at getting outside the nine dots of Figure 9.7 is vital. Processes can always be improved, but sometimes it needs a completely new way provided by simply asking the question: 'Why do we do it this way?'

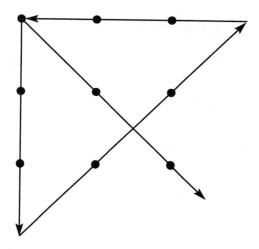

Fig 9.11 Answer to nine dots puzzle

10

Monitoring Performance Improvement

How do you know when you're really winning?

- **The reasons for using cost of quality models to measure performance improvement**
- **The prevention, appraisal, failure approach to cost of quality**
- **Running a pilot study**
- **Using the process cost model approach to measure process improvement**

INTRODUCTION

Throughout the book so far the need to set targets has been stressed, and the need to measure and monitor your performance, both as an organisation and as an individual. One of the most difficult measurement systems to set up is the 'simple' *cost of quality model* using the prevention, appraisal and failure approach. Once established, this provides an overall picture of progress and helps to see where the implementation of change is being most effective. As your programme of change progresses, so you will begin to employ the more sophisticated process cost model in planning improvement and monitoring the changes. As you do so, your dependence on the initial model will fall away. Typically, this will take two to three years.

But what are these 'models'?

As far back as 1981, a British Standard was published, BS 6143:1981 entitled 'A Guide to the Determination and Use of Quality-Related Costs'. This used the prevention, appraisal, failure approach. As total quality and the concept of zero errors and defects became more widely accepted, the standard was reviewed and improved, eventually being re-issued in 1990 and 1991 as two models, the more traditional Prevention, Appraisal and Failure (PAF) Model (BS 6143: 1990, part 2) and a new Process Cost Model (BS 6143: 1991, part 1) methodology.

THE SIGNIFICANCE OF QUALITY-RELATED COSTS

Quality-related activities have a huge impact on the success of any business. The cost of those activities has an even bigger impact on company profitability, competitiveness and, ultimately, existence. It is often said that organisations compete on three things, quality, delivery and price. However, it can be easily demonstrated that *price* competitiveness and an organisation's ability to improve and widen the range of the activities it *delivers* is dependent on the cost of achieving the desired level of *quality*.

A portion of any organisation's total operating costs is earmarked for meeting its quality objectives. That is those elements of its total costs which are necessary for delivering the products and services customers require to the desired quality level.

In 1985, the National Economic Development Office (NEDO), task force on quality and standards, chaired by Sir Frederick Warner, estimated quality-related costs to be between 10 and 20 per cent of the total sales value of a business. The lower figure corresponded to the annual cost (£6 billion) within UK manufacturing industry alone. Further reports from all types of organisation indicate that quality-related costs commonly ranged from 5 per cent to 25 per cent of company sales turnover. As you can see, quality-related costs are very large, often greater than an organisation's total net profit, and therefore their management is paramount.

The costs will obviously depend on the type of industry, business, situation or service that is provided. They will also vary depending on the view taken by each organisation as to what is or is not a quality-related cost, its approach to continuous quality improvement and the extent to which it is practised by all departments and people within the organisation.

Because 95 per cent of these costs are usually expended on *appraisal* and *failure*, which are seen to add little to the value of a product or service, and because the failure costs at least may be regarded as avoidable, their measurement is often ignored as seeming to have no relevance to quality improvement. The permanent reduction of costs due to failure within the organisation can also lead to substantial reduction in necessary appraisal costs. Evidence from research by the University of Manchester Institute of Science and Technology, suggests that quality-related costs may be reduced by one third of their present level within a period of three years by a commitment to the process of continuous improvement, removing failure and waste from the organisation permanently.

Unnecessary and avoidable costs make goods and services *necessarily* more expensive and this in turn affects competitiveness. Organisations which can control such avoidable costs have much greater flexibility in their cost base and can make significant step changes in their pricing policies without greatly affecting profitability. Measuring the costs of quality-related activities allows them to be expressed in the same management language, i.e. money, as marketing, research, development and operations. In turn, this serves to identify the importance of quality-related activities to corporate health, just as all the other activities. In this way, the effect of quality-related activities on an overall business performance will influence behaviour and attitudes towards quality improvement.

BENEFITS OF QUALITY COST REPORTING

Through the use of quality cost reports, attention can be focused on all areas of high expenditure and potential cost reduction opportunities. Quality cost reports allow the measurement of performance and provide a basis of comparison between products, services, processes, departments, quality improvement groups and divisions. Such measurement and reports can reveal the quirks and anomalies in cost allocations and standards which otherwise would remain undetected by other methods.

The analysis of quality-related costs has been known to uncover fraudulent activities taking place within an organisation and avoid the dumping of embarrassing after-sales costs under quality-related headings, warranty costs, service on repairs, policy adjustments and so on.

Perhaps the most important reason for understanding and measuring the economic factors of quality is that measurement is the first step towards control. Knowledge of the costs enables business decisions about quality to be made in an objective, rather than an emotional manner. They permit analysis and evaluation of expenditure on projects devoted to continuous improvement. Also, they may be used to monitor quality improvement performance and enable budgets to be set and levels of control to be improved. By featuring quality-related cost reports regularly within management accounts the cost of quality and the value of real quality improvements can be kept in the spotlight.

Definitions

We have already indicated that some quality-related costs can be considered avoidable, *appraisal costs* and *failure costs*. For this reason they are often ignored. There are unavoidable or essential quality-related costs, those which can be categorised as *prevention costs*.

Simply, *quality-related costs* are the total expenditure incurred by an organisation in error or defect prevention and appraisal activities, plus the losses and additional costs incurred due to internal and external failure.

In most organisations, an important part of any activity when nearing completion is to ask the question '... have we done it right this time?' This is *appraisal*. Appraisal can be formal, in the form of inspection or informal, by way of self-administered checks. Often it is too late to be asking this question and the answer is 'no'. This is *failure*. Usually we can do something about it and, we refer to it then as *internal failure*. We can repeat the task, scrap what we have done and start again; we can carry out some form of rectification, but all at an additional cost. Sometimes we forget to ask the question at the right time and the customer tells us that the answer is 'no'. This is *external failure*.

To minimise the likelihood of the answer to the original question, '... have we done it right this time?' being 'no', many organisations engage in a variety of activities aimed at ensuring that the desired quality is achieved, right first time. This is *prevention*.

Traditionally, these have been the main considerations when focusing on quality-related costs, but they ignore the costs of the process itself with all of its own in-built waste and unnecessary activity.

In the new *process cost model,* costs are divided between the *cost of conformance,* and the *cost of non-conformance.* The first is the intrinsic cost of providing the product or service to the required standard using the specified process effectively. The *cost of non-conformance* is all those costs including, wasted time, materials, capacity associated with the process and the correction of the process when not carried out effectively.

Why two models?

In the initial stages of the development of a quality-focused organisational culture, more investment is required in *prevention* and *appraisal* in order to make significant reductions in the cost of *failure*. However, this is ultimately too restrictive. As we have already identified, this methodology ignores the process itself and cannot for long support a culture which focuses more on processes. When an organisation becomes more attuned to a customer-centred process approach, so the only valid partition of quality costs is seen as that between *cost of conformance* and *cost of non-conformance* because both provide the opportunity for continuous improvement.

The traditional PAF model does imply an acceptable level of quality. This cannot be compatible with the philosophy of total quality, whatever the organisation's model, because the only maxim accepted by all of the quality gurus is the total and long-term commitment to continuous improvement. However, in the initial stages of a quality improvement initiative, the traditional approach is worthwhile. It provides a simple methodology which helps to demonstrate the size of the opportunity for quality improvement in financial terms. This in its turn provides objective evidence on which to base decisions on the size of investments in prevention and quality improvement training. It also provides a simple benchmark with which to measure progress in the early months and years. Through the activity of developing a simple quality cost model and associated reports, significant cost areas which require improvement action will be highlighted, and again decisions, this time on where to start the continuous improvement programme, can be based on well-researched facts.

As time passes, and the organisation becomes more interested in process improvement, so there will be more call on the process cost approach. Gradually this will take over from the PAF approach as the organisation becomes more sophisticated in its understanding of the effect of the control of quality-related costs on organisational performance and results.

QUALITY-RELATED COSTS AND CONTINUOUS IMPROVEMENT

It is generally accepted that if more resources are invested in prevention and to a small extent initially in appraisal, then failure costs will decrease significantly over a fairly short period. If we consider just the PAF model, we can see that there will come a time when to increase investment in prevention will, in theory, increase total quality costs. Thus suggesting that there is an optimum cost of quality.

When BS 6143 was first issued, this idea of an optimum cost of quality was still being advanced, using Figure 10.1 to reinforce the argument. However, in the 1990 revision of the standard there is no reference to this notion, and they advance an alternative model which demonstrates the results of recent studies (Figure 10.2). These suggest that despite the different patterns which vary from company to company, generally, organisations will see an increase in appraisal costs as quality awareness increases. Then, as appraisal together with investigation points to areas where improvements can be made, more is spent on prevention. As the preventative action takes hold, so the prevention, appraisal and failure cost proportions realign and all costs reduce.

This is more in harmony with the opinions of many quality specialists who from real experience point out that:

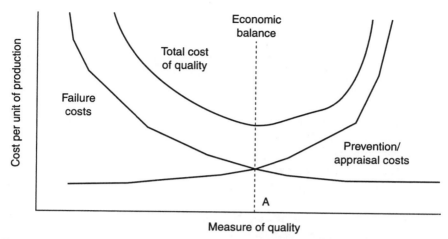

Fig 10.1 Traditional prevention, appraisal and failure (PAF) model

Fig 10.2 New, contrasting approach to the pattern of quality costs

- the idea of an economic balance or an optimum quality level conflicts with the widely-accepted philosophy of zero errors and defects being practical;

- if in fact there is an optimum economic level for quality it lies much closer to, or very near, perfection;

- the acceptance of the idea of an optimum quality level may well inhibit the process of continuous improvement;

- in the optimum quality level model, the cost curves of prevention, appraisal and failure suggest that for a small investment in prevention and/or appraisal, a major reduction in failure costs will result. In practice it is not as dramatic and it could lead to false hopes of success.

If we analyse the results of quality cost models, typically we find in the majority of organisations the proportions of quality-related costs do align more or less with the proportions shown in the left hand column in Figure 10.3, which also coincide with the findings of the NEDO task force, i.e. 95 per cent *appraisal* and *failure*. As more resources are invested in *prevention* and *appraisal* so the real cost of failure does fall and the organisation's reputation for getting things right first time is increased.

The proportion of *appraisal* to *failure* does vary from organisation to organisation and the highest proportion of *appraisal* costs is found to occur in the financial and legal services sectors. It is in those sectors that we also find the proportion of total quality-related costs to total sales revenue at the highest, in some instances as high as 37.5 per cent.

Analysing the results of quality-related cost investigations is a key tool in *process improvement*. It provides a particularly useful pointer to identifying the top priorities for improvement action, as well as a benchmark to determine the degree of improvement achieved. Once we have the outline quality-related costs using the PAF model and we have an understanding of the process costs we can describe the process improvement options in the way described in Figure 10.4.

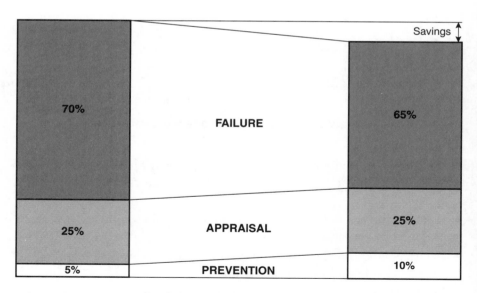

Fig 10.3 Results of traditional prevention, appraisal and failure (PAF) model

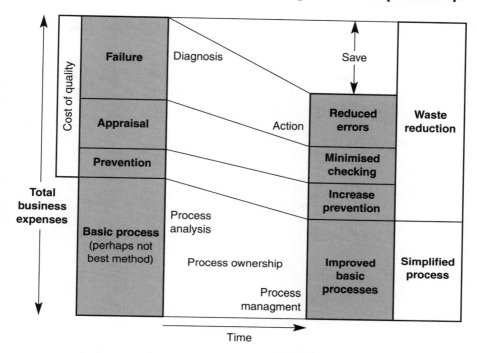

Fig 10.4 Quality-related costs and continuous improvement

USING QUALITY-RELATED COST ANALYSIS IN CONTINUOUS IMPROVEMENT

Increasing *prevention* activity reduces failure and the need for inspection (*appraisal*). IBM has estimated that for every pound invested in *prevention*, it has saved £10 on errors otherwise picked up by inspection or £100 through *internal failure*.

Figure 10.4 demonstrates the need for the model to be extended through the use of the *process cost* model to provide additional information upon which to base improvements to basic processes. The simple PAF model provides the basis for failure diagnosis and natural problem-solving action by work teams. This will lead to a reduction in waste and error rate. With the addition of the process cost model analysis, team purpose analysis and departmental purpose analysis can take place with real costs available. This leads to increased process ownership and eventually to process management.

ESTABLISHING A SIMPLE QUALITY COST MODEL

The methodology of this model was proposed as far back as 1956 by Dr Armand Feigenbaum, but not really developed until the early 1970s and was first recognised by the American Society of Quality Control (ASQC) in 1974. This was the basis of BS 6143 when first issued in 1981. Its use, as we have already indicated, is at its best at the start of a quality improvement programme when it provides an overview of quality-related costs, and acts as the initial focus for cost effective improvement efforts. One of its more practical properties is that it can be made as coarse or as fine a measure as the organisation desires and can be used to establish the costs for the whole organisation or for separate divisions and departments.

The quality cost elements will differ between companies and industries, but it is important to note that any of the elements of quality-related costs used in the model must:

- be relevant to the improvement process;
- be capable of being measured consistently.

To maintain this consistency, management has to decide which costs will be included and within that, which will be attributed to day-to-day operational control and set against operational costs and which will be identified as solely being measures for the purpose of quality assurance. It is the assignment of these costs to the various headings within the model which often proves the most difficult task.

The BS 6143: part 2, 1990 provides a checklist to help with this analysis. However, more than half of the checklist is devoted to prevention costs and to appraisal costs. This is clearly disproportionate to the percentages of actual quality costs where, as we have already seen, the majority fall under the headings of internal or external failure. In addition, small companies have particular difficulty in identifying prevention costs at the outset of any programme. Therefore cost elements specific to an organisation, especially with regard to failure, need to be identified by department and by process using a brainstorming approach. By this method it is not unusual to find the majority of cost elements identified as failure (see Figure 10.5 later).

Applying the PAF model to identify cost elements

Let us just look for a moment at what we mean by the four key headings of *internal failure*, *external failure*, *appraisal* and *prevention*.

Internal failure costs are the costs arising within an organisation due to non-conformities or defects at any stage in the quality loop once materials have been accepted, such as scrap, rework, failure analysis, re-inspection and retesting, redesign, concessions, downgrading, down-time and subcontractor fault.

External failure costs are those arising after supply of service or delivery of product to the customer due to any non-conformities or defects which may include the costs of claims against warranty, dealing with complaints, rejected and returned product, concessions, recall costs, product liability and ultimately the loss of sales due to customers going elsewhere.

Appraisal costs are those costs incurred in initially ascertaining the conformance of the product or service to the quality required (they do not include costs of rework or re-inspection following failure). These costs include all verification and inspection including pre-production, acceptance testing, inspection and test equipment, external analyses, field tests, stock evaluation and the storage of quality records.

Prevention costs are usually the most difficult category to identify initially, but they include the costs of quality planning, calibration and maintenance, supplier assurance, quality training and auditing and the quality improvement programmes themselves, i.e. all costs of any actions taken to investigate, prevent or reduce the risk of getting it wrong.

When setting out on initial data collection, start with *failure*, then *appraisal* and when you have gained some experience of collection and analysis, turn your attention to *prevention*.

The cost elements of *failure* may be better considered in the way demonstrated in Figure 10.5 (overleaf).

Once you have decided on the cost element categories and have carried out some analysis to decide into which of the four main areas they are to be put, the data collection can begin. Following the initial collection of data from local and functional areas, further analysis is normally necessary, especially if the organisation does not already have a departmental costing system that will accommodate the quality costs being identified.

Specifying quality-related costs

In building a simple quality cost model you must ensure that the cost elements identified are appropriate to the organisation in terms of quality improvements required. There is little point in taking time to measure the costs incurred by outdated equipment if that equipment is to be replaced in the short-term. Similarly, outdated processes or services which are to be discontinued can be ignored, as can insignificant costs which, although irritating, would not provide much benefit to the organisation if improvements, even large ones, could be made.

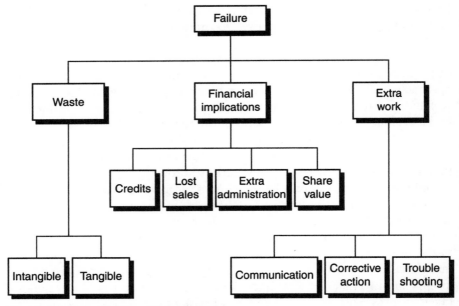

Fig 10.5 Internal failure cost elements

Any quality costs steering group must initially decide on how it will be consistent in categorising the four main groups, i.e. prevention, appraisal, internal and external failure. It almost certainly will be necessary to record some quality costs in a subsidiary ledger or memorandum account. For this reason the management accountant is a vital member of the quality cost group.

Expenditures resulting from most, if not all four categories, will cut across conventional, functional, as well as accounting boundaries in most organisations. Therefore it is important to establish the purpose of the exercise at the start. If, for example, the main purpose is to identify high cost problem areas in order to promote team problem-solving and continuous improvement, then approximate costs in many known problem areas will suffice. However, if the purpose is to set cost reduction targets on quality-related costs, then it may be necessary to identify and measure all contributing elements so costs are reduced and not simply transferred elsewhere.

It is also important at the outset to take input from the management accountant regarding the elements to be included in each group and what data sources are available to provide consistent information. Input from the management accountant is also invaluable when it comes to the coding of cost data to make tabulation easier.

The aim in setting up the specification is that all cost data be reported by codes or events, permitting simple interpretation by the accountants into real cost data, using standard and consistent sources. In some instances, it may be necessary to develop synthetic data or make expense allocation arbitrarily, but in all these instances the quality costing group must be in agreement and should be able to explain the reasons behind its decisions.

Eventually, quality cost data will be collected by all operational departments and reported regularly.

Departmental responsibilities

The accounting department should assume responsibility for the collection and collation of the raw quality cost data, allocation of these costs to agreed activities and standard cost elements and for providing comparative bases for quality cost assessment. The accounting department should also be responsible for the production of an operating report which matches the regular accountancy reporting periods.

The quality assurance department should analyse quality-related costs; co-ordinate activity between departments to achieve cost objectives; establish cost reduction and control policies; arbitrate on responsibility for quality failure costs. It should also be responsible for interpreting the regular reports issued by the accounting department and issuing commentaries on them.

Meanwhile, all operations departments will be responsible for collecting data or encoding; deciding the feasibility of improvements following reports from the quality department; increasing the awareness of individuals regarding quality-related activities within their sphere of operations; and for becoming involved in the whole process of continuous improvement.

Analysis of specification data

In building the specification we have to consider not only which heading a particular cost element falls into, but exactly what the element involves, how it may be calculated and finally where a consistent source of data may be obtained. The source may be actual cost data already collected or synthetic data which has to be developed. Determining contents and data source will require considerable analysis which should be carried out in a systematic manner.

Analysis requires five steps. The first of these is to determine the costs that are directly attributable to the quality function. Items such as payroll costs for specific quality functioning employees, overhead apportionment and administration costs, depreciation of specialised quality control and assessment equipment, etc.

Step two is to identify those costs that are not directly the responsibility of the quality function but which should be counted as part of the total quality-related costs of the organisation. These will normally be incurred by other departments, but because we do not wish to make any formal accounting transfers, a memorandum account of these items may need to be made and apportionment agreed.

These first two steps will determine items normally under the headings prevention and appraisal. The next three steps are concerned with failure costs.

The third step is to determine and establish memorandum accounts for internal costs of budgeted failures, that is where budgets are established on the basis of not accepting failure in some form. This may, for example, be in production where in order to produce a hundred of something, an extra ten will be budgeted to ensure that a hundred meet the quality requirement. If the figures are small in this area they may be ignored, but generally it is worth including them in any trial period and then on the basis of experience their inclusion can be continued or discarded as appropriate.

Step four will identify the internal costs of failures not allowed for in step three, i.e. the unplanned failure. Related costs may include materials that have been scrapped, cost of rework, etc. Usually, these costs are hidden away in overall figures for a department and almost certainly special analysis and a memorandum account will need to be established.

The final step is often full of surprises. Its purpose is to determine the cost of the failures after the change of ownership throughout a process. These costs are often caused by barriers or black holes in the processes and the costs will include time spent by both the quality department and the function involved in investigating failures, reworking during process, delay and wasted time. They may also include the costs of other departments such as marketing, customer services and accounts. These costs that are rarely identified in traditional systems. Here, initial estimates may be used and a memorandum account kept to check from time to time the veracity of the initial values. Care must be taken here not to count things already accounted for under step one.

Data sources

As we have established, it is important to involve management accounts in this exercise and although there are no established rules for searching out date you will find valuable sources in the following documents:

- payroll analyses;
- production expense reports;

- scrap or waste reports;
- rework and rectification authorisations;
- travel expense claims;
- production or service costs information;
- field repair, replacement and warranty reports, including concessions;
- inspection and test records;
- material review records;
- non-conformance reports;
- design or specification changes and concession data.

These items, while not exhaustive, have proven to be valuable sources of the necessary data for this exercise.

Quality cost reports

Once the initial data, both real and synthetic has been developed and the specification finalised, it is vital that it is maintained in this format for some considerable period. Any changes found necessary must be agreed by the quality costing group, which is responsible for the model and its reports.

Reports on quality cost models which use the PAF methodology are also fairly simple statements. An example of a typical quality cost report format is shown in Figure 10.6 which also shows some typical data. Such reports of plain data would normally be produced by accounts, but on their own are of little management value and need some interpretation which is best done by the quality function. In this context, report design is important and some time should be devoted to agreeing the best format for presentation. Pictures, we are told, are worth a thousand words, therefore suitable pie charts and graphs need to be developed and agreed at the outset in order to show improvement, or otherwise, over time. It may be that some reports would be more meaningful if broken down by department or function. As the programme progresses, individual reports by improvement project and specific problem area might be appropriate. But once again consistency of approach must be stressed.

In reporting quality costs trends, ratios using standard bases understood by most managers are of considerable value. It is recommended that at least three measurement bases be used initially, relating to quality costs. They should represent the business from different viewpoints and be sensitive to business change, e.g. internal failure costs related to total labour or direct labour; total failure costs related to total manufacturing costs; total quality costs related to net sales value or perhaps using a value added base; and total quality-related costs related to a measure of manufacturing activity unaffected by fluctuation in sales or purchased goods and services (see Figure 10.5).

Once again a cautionary note on consistency must be made here. Measurement bases are only as good as the methods for keeping them consistent. The inclusion of such ratios with the reports is invaluable. From this report, managers should be able to identify critical areas where attention is needed and should be able to draw comparisons from total quality cost data displayed. A further help to their understanding is to introduce ranking of costs of particular problem areas. Appropriate use of Pareto analysis will assist in identifying the most costly and frequent errors and help managers to prioritise their efforts.

PILOT STUDY

Once the initial specification has been agreed, the group must plan and carry out a pilot study to determine feasibility and reliability of the model. The pilot should be run for about three months and may not necessarily cover the whole model. It is often better to choose cost areas where the pilot study is likely to be successful. The time period should not be open-ended. Three months should be sufficient time to establish viability before developing the model further. The quality cost elements used in the pilot must be specific to the organisation and should cover all the relevant categories.

Success, as with all studies, is dependent on many factors, but particularly the way the programme is set up in the initial stages. To this end, the analysis of the different cost elements and the specification, contents and data sources, are critical factors.

Management commitment is also essential to the success of the pilot as well as the design of the model itself. They must be aware of the quality-related cost procedures that are involved and to this end a certain amount of training and promotion in awareness is required. Managers must be willing to promote the quality cost awareness actively throughout the organisation and be prepared to participate in initiatives to take action on the improvement requirements highlighted by the quality costing activities. This may also require additional training and coaching resource.

When the full programme is introduced, it provides the motivating force for organisation-wide process improvement and the elimination of waste. To take full advantage of this opportunity, the whole workforce must be fully briefed, not only in the reasons for collecting the necessary data but on how to work in teams to solve the problems highlighted and

COST OF QUALITY

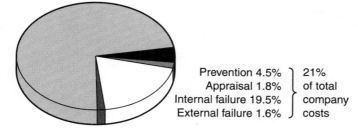

Prevention 4.5% ⎫ 21%
Appraisal 1.8% ⎪ of total
Internal failure 19.5% ⎬ company
External failure 1.6% ⎭ costs

	Activity	Cost of quality (£000)	% of total expenditure
Prevention	On the job training	75	
	Process definition	40	
	Preventative maintenance	163	
	Production planning	36	
	Supplier invoicing	10	
	Other	57	
	Total	**38**	**4.5%**
Appraisal	Ouality audits	12	
	Checking output	80	
	DP checking	20	
	Checking drawings	30	
	Other	12	
	Total	**154**	**1.8%**
Internal failure	Unplanned maintenance	390	
	Downtime	594	
	Stopping production	30	
	Outwork	110	
	Spoilage	227	
	Overtime because of failure	118	
	Supervision because of troubleshooting	115	
	Other	46	
	Total	**1630**	**19.2%**
External failure	Dealing with complaints and delays	77	
	Requests	17	
	Visit about errors	28	
	Other	15	
	Total	**137**	**1.6%**
Overall cost of quality		**2,302**	**27.1%**

Fig 10.6 Typical cost quality report

to implement change. To achieve maximum benefit, a strategically-planned programme of training and facilitating will be required.

Figure 10.7 gives a checklist for a simple cost of quality model.

USING THE PROCESS COST MODEL

All organisations which aspire to world class performance or a total quality culture must manage the *processes* of their organisation, in addition to the functions. The understanding and management of processes is a fundamental building block in achieving these aspirations, whether the organisation is in manufacturing or service, a profit maker or a charity. Additionally, it must be recognised that every person within an organisation operates within and contributes to a process, everything we do is a process. To achieve world class performance, every process within an organisation must be identified, described (and mapped) and have an identified *process owner* who is responsible for the effectiveness of the process.

As we have seen, the PAF model approach to identifying and analysing quality-related costs suggests that certain, identifiable, costs are in some way related to the 'quality' of the end result of any activity or process. In contrast, within world class organisations where a TQM culture exists, all business activity is related to processes. Therefore, if we wish to identify and analyse quality-related costs, then the model we use should reflect the total costs of each process rather than the arbitrarily-defined elements of quality-related costs used in the PAF model.

Ultimately, the only valid partitioning of quality-related cost elements is that between the *costs of conformance* (that is the cost of the process including the elements of prevention and appraisal built into it) and the *costs of non-conformance* (the costs of failure resulting from not performing the process, as specified, right first time).

As we have already discussed, both the cost of conformance and the costs of non-conformance are capable of improvement and reduction, the first by the development and improvement of the process through improved efficiency and the elimination of wasteful activities which add no value, and non-conformance cost elements by reduction of waste through the elimination of failure via a variety of methods.

The management of processes may be considered at a variety of different levels within the organisation, ranging from a small individual activity or task to a major business process such as purchasing, production planning or order handling.

Form a project team of middle managers and supervisors (including the management accountant if possible) representing each functional area.	❏
Explain task to develop a quality cost model and the background to methodology and use.	❏
Carry out a brainstorming session of all well-known and not so well-known, internal and, external failures. Be prepared for surprises and emphasise the need to table the generally-accepted failures.	❏
Assign each team member to carry out a team brainstorm within their functional area to determine the most important and common failures from the general staff view point.	❏
Analyse results as a team and identify categories	❏
Decide content of model in terms of headline problems. Do not agonise over trivia. Start with internal and external failure and then move back through *appraisal* which should be viewed as a reducible cost and then to *prevention* which can be difficult to define in the early stages of building a model.	❏
Identify standard source data available reliably from accounts department.	❏
Set up data collection programme to determine key cost standards and to establish synthetic costings to be used in the model.	❏
Plan and carry out pilot study to determine feasibility and reliability of model and consistency of data collection from standard sources. Run pilot for about three months or until reproducible data can be produced for three consecutive months.	❏
Agree final content of quality cost model and report style.	❏
Team meets every six months to review accuracy and content.	❏
Unless significant changes occur, there should not be a need to revise estimated and synthetic costs more often than annually.	❏

Fig 10.7 Checklist to prepare a simple cost of quality model

If cultural change is to take place within an organisation committed to continuous improvement, process owners, individuals, supervisors and even the managing director, need to be able to monitor all the cost elements of the processes they are responsible for in order to take the appropriate action to ensure that the costs are minimised.

As the programme of initiatives to reduce the high cost areas highlighted by the use of the PAF model take, so the pressure to understand the cost elements of the processes themselves will increase. This in itself will generate the need to apply the process cost model approach and eventually will replace the PAF model in controlling the quality-related costs of the organisation. Both methods can be used simultaneously. However the experience gained in preparing a PAF model first, especially in specification and pilot, does help towards early success with a process cost approach.

Using the process cost model (BS 6143, part 1)

The preparation of a process cost model according to BS 6143, part 1, 1990, has three stages:

- identify all the *inputs*, *outputs*, *controls* and *resources* of the process under consideration by preparing a simple *process model*;
- develop a *process map* or flowchart for the process;
- identify the cost elements of the process and ultimate sources of cost data.

As with the PAF model, the key to providing meaningful cost reports and analyses is to be found in the early specification stage. Carefully-considered decisions must be made on identifying all cost elements; whether actual or synthetic costs are to be used; how synthetic costs are to be determined; the means of calculating each element of cost; and a reliable source for the cost data.

Preparing a process model

In this first stage, a block diagram showing all the elements affecting the process will be prepared. This model helps to focus attention on the need for the process as well. Because we are often looking at a process which is part of a much larger process, it is important at this stage to clearly define the start and finish point of the process by establishing boundaries. Use natural break points wherever possible.

Once the boundaries have been defined, the next step is to identify all of the *outputs* of the process and the *customers* for them. Having identified all of the outputs and their customers, the next step is to identify all of the *inputs* to the process and their *suppliers*. In addition to inputs and outputs, processes also have *controls* and *resources* which also must be identified together with the *sources* of these possible constraints on improvement. An example of the steps in the preparation of a *process model* is shown in Figure 10.8 and Figure 10.9.

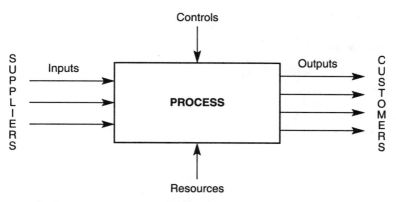

Fig 10.8 Foundation of the process cost model

The second stage requires the mapping or flowcharting of the process. It may have already been carried out; if not, a process map must be produced. It is the analysis of the process map together with the process model which will help identify the cost elements. The methodology for process mapping and making flowcharts is covered in chapter 12. One element to stress at this point is that to prepare a complete process map requires the assembly of a team of people who between them know the full range of activities making up the process.

Once the process map is complete and everyone agrees that it is actually what takes place (not what a supervisor hopes takes place), then you can start the final stage of identifying the key activities within the process and to analyse the cost elements in terms of:

- people;
- equipment;
- materials and methods;
- environment.

Identifying quality-related cost elements and their sources

Each process contains a number of key activities which must be identified. The cost of conformance and the cost of non-conformance for each key activity must then be identified and agreed. The results of these deliberations can be tabulated using the format shown in Figure 10.10.

Having identified the cost elements for the key activities, progress can be made in the preparation of the cost report and specification of cost data source, using the format in Figure 10.11.

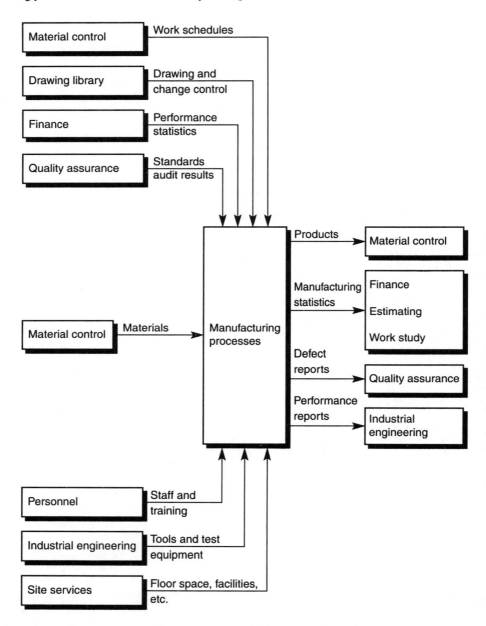

Fig 10.9 Typical inputs and outputs of manufacturing processes

Cost model for a manufacturing department		
Key activity	Cost of conformance	Cost of non-conformance
Planning, production engineering work study, cost control. materials and process laboratory	Part cost	Part cost (effect ot engineering change, planning errors. etc.)
Production inspection costs	'Good' hours booked	Reinspection/retest/and test fault-finding
Test gear depreciation, calibration and preventative maintenance	Total cost	
Breakdowns		Total cost
Production costs	'Good' hours booked	Rework
Material costs	Estimated cost	Scrap cost, overspend
Waiting time		Total cost
Cost of work held due to shortages		Total cost

Fig 10.10 Elements of costs of conformance and costs of non-conformance

As can be seen, the cost report contains a complete list of the identified cost elements of each activity in terms of conformance and non-conformance costs and specifies:

- all inputs, outputs, controls and resources of the process being considered;
- whether actual or synthetic costs are being used;
- the means of calculation for each element of cost;
- the source of the data.

As with the preparation of the PAF model, it is valuable to have the management accountant as part of the team considering the establishment of the report. Management accountants can provide valuable advice on the composition of synthetic costs and the reliability of actual cost data.

Improving the process

Once a process cost report has been established, a programme of quality improvement activities should be developed on the basis of the information.

PROCESS COST REPORT

PROCESS Production Department   **PROCESS OWNER** Manufacturing Manager   Date

Process conformance	Cost			Process non-conformance	Cost			Cost data source
	Actual	Synthetic	£		Actual	Synthetic	£	
People Assembly, inspection and test	✔							Produced hours × hourly rate from accounts package
				Hours taken of rework, reinspection, retest	✔			Excess codes: hours × hourly rate from accounts package
				Waiting time	✔			Excess codes: hours × hourly rate from accounts package
Equipment Cost of capital equipment to carry out work, i.e. depreciation, calibration, maintenance, chronos	✔							Accounts package: capital assets inventory × (manufacturing efficiency)
				Cost of capital equipment to carry out rework, etc.	✔			Accounts package: capital assets inventory × (1 − manufacturing efficiency)
Environment Floor space, maintenance facilities,	✔							Accounts package: (floor space, site services, telephones, site administration, maintenance) × manufacturing efficiency
				Floor space, etc. for rework				Accounts package: (floor space, site services, telephones, site administration, maintenance) x (1 − manufacturing efficiency)
Materials and methods Purchased material and material handling and packaging	✔							Cost estimates
				Scrap, contingencies material price variance	✔			Scrap report
Task allocation, supervision of process progressing (NOTE: Processing information provided by industrial engineering)	✔							Accounts package: (supervision, progress labour costs) x y%*
				Fault finding guides, cost of change, implementation, on the job training	✔			Accounts package: (supervision, progress labour costs) × (1 − y)%*
Total process conformance cost				Total process non-conformance cost				

Prepared by ....

*y is the agreed proportion of the costs being considered.

Fig 10.11 Typical cost report for a manufacturing department

Priorities can be established and the process owner should be responsible for establishing initiatives to consider improvements using teams and establish reliable methods of monitoring the resultant changes.

Decisions on whether process design or elimination of waste is the first priority can be made after consideration of the initial balance between cost of conformance and cost of non-conformance given in the report. The ability to understand the cost elements of both the basic process and the additional quality-related costs provides much greater scope for improvement and faster return on the investment in the programme.

Now that is the technical method and a series of methodologies covered which will need to mastered over time. However I am sure you are still saying:

'How do you know when TQM is really happening?'

Well, here are some pointers to look for to indicate when your organisation is really on the way towards the total quality culture you seek:

- When top managers begin to bite their own bullets – that is when the senior team takes ownership of some of the problems of their making instead of trying to shift the blame. When you are finger-pointing, remember for every finger you point at someone else there are three pointing back at you – if you do not believe me, do it and look at your own hand!

- When everyone in the organisation understands the concepts and their personal responsibility for quality – want to know if they continue to meet their customers' requirements, and actually meet with them regularly to discuss how they are doing.

- When it is a daily subject of discussion amongst management. Top of every agenda at meetings.

- When people see that it is what they are paid to do, so there is time for it.

- When employees in general start talking about their internal customers and doing something about it – customer–supplier agreements are set up without supervisors and managers being involved and managers relate to their subordinates as customers.

- When the use of quality tools and techniques is part of 'business as usual'. Cause and effect diagrams are visible, brainstorming is automatic and everyone counts what is happening because they are looking for improvements.

- When everyone is involved in contributing , either individually or collectively, to continuous improvement – you are reaching your targets with regard to numbers of people involved in improvement teams (target 100 per cent).

- When progress is being measured – using regular critical reviews against the key improvement targets and using cost of quality models as well.
- When people are responsible for checking the quality of their own work, you will have stopped formal inspection. All people make their own checks, even measurements and laboratory tests, in which they have been trained and feel confident to carry out.
- When top managers re-commit and re-dedicate themselves to total quality management after things have got tough and the temptation is to back off.

11

A Recipe for Being Truly World Class

Developing a consistently reproducible culture that could be transplanted from organisation to organisation and from country to country (the way you *do things around here).*

- Developing your own business philosophy
- Anticipation; innovation; excellence
- Documenting clearly your total vision

INTRODUCTION

In the introduction and in chapter 1 we considered the unique characteristics of a world class organisation, those things which set them apart from other organisations, even apart from the good ones. Establishing an effective total quality culture, a structure which is based on customer-focused teamwork and process-oriented management is not sufficient in itself to be world class.

So what else do you need?

All truly world class organisations have developed their own unique formula for creating continuing growth and success. Some organisations such as the Mars Group, for example have created 'scale economy, branded businesses' around the world, consistently producing growth and high returns on capital employed. By applying their unique formula to both the confectionery and pet food markets, Mars has created an internationally transferable business system, driven by low-cost manufacture, from scale economies of operation; high service levels to customers through sophisticated marketing and logistics; total quality, through best practice execution skills and superior product value delivery to the consumer, allowing sustained premium pricing.

Other companies which have their own unique formula for sustained growth and wealth creation include Toyota and Nissan (built around their own style of lean production), Microsoft (software innovation), RTZ (mineral dominance), Riverwood (supplying to markets it creates from the resources it creates) and nearer to home Caradon (developing underperforming businesses). Each has its own unique way of continually motivating and enhancing the performance of its constituent parts through a common operating strategy which can be applied to any function, process, department, subsidiary or constituent operating organisation. It is sometimes referred to as a *business philosophy* or *the way we do things around here*, it is a blend of skills, culture and process application.

During the initial stages of implementing a total quality programme you will have many opportunities to gather data from all the stakeholders as to their vision of the type of organisation into which they see you developing. The external and internal surveys you conduct will also give you valuable information, if you ask the right questions.

Developing a business philosophy takes time. It will to some extent be an evolutionary process and for total acceptance must be a participative process. However, the eventual formula will be agreed by the senior managers who will lead its implementation.

As an essential element of establishing a philosophy, organisations must take a very long view. They must identify those factors that are not only critical to current success but that will continue to be critical over time.

Joel Barker in his book *Future Edge* asserts that there are three keys to future continuing success for any organisation. They are:

- anticipation;
- innovation;
- excellence.

He goes on to say that he lists excellence at the end of the list because for the far future into the next century, excellence (or total quality management) will be the base for the future. He suggests that on its own it may give organisations a competitive edge for only the next decade. After that it will become the necessary price of entry, and I certainly agree with him.

But what are the areas where *anticipation* and *innovation* will make the difference?

Casting our minds back to Dr Deming, continuous improvement is required to anticipate what customers will want in the future in order to provide the opportunity to delight them again and again. The competitive edge, as we have also already discussed, will come from *breakthroughs* in our thinking or innovation. The areas where clearly you can make a difference are therefore to be found within the world class model built up in chapter 1 and the development of the individual elements which make up the core

(Figure 11.1). Each of the *environment creators* will be revisited each year, developing them to meet the new strategic plans of the organisation, the distinctively unique operating strategy comes from the development of the continuous development of the core.

The core comprises:

- a commitment to a customer focus;
- a process-oriented structure;
- a system to manage those processes;
- goal-driven measures of performance cascading down the organisation;
- properly managed and resourced teamwork;

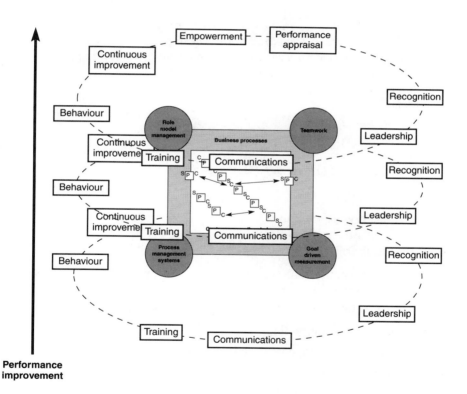

Fig 11.1 World class organisation model

- visible and active, role-model management leading the establishment of common values, practices and behaviour by example.

It is each of these which should be examined in the finest detail, one at a time, to establish a unique formula that can be worked on to produce the world class organisation. For each element you must identify the components where *anticipation* of future requirements and *innovation* are essential for future, continuing success and which must be dependably, and consistently, reproducible. This should be approached in the same way as a strategic business plan. For each element ask the key question:

- *What is our total vision for this element?*

followed by;

- *How do we see it now?*
- *Where will it be if we continue with present practices?*
- *What are the current strengths and weaknesses?*
- *Where are we vulnerable (what are the opportunities and threats)?*
- *What must we do to bridge the gap in terms of:*
  - *manpower?*
  - *growth?*
  - *organisation?*
  - *finance?*
  - *facilities?*
  - *development and research to stay ahead?*

Each time you should ask:

- *what is this organisation to achieve?*
- *where do we want to be and by when?*
- *what goals must we set to get there?*

In addition, to ensure that the organisation keeps up the momentum for change and maintains leadership in *innovation*, the core skills required by *all* managers to sustain world class performance. Typically, these would include:

- customer-focused marketing;
- human resource management and development;
- supply chain management;
- business cycle and economic cycle management;
- pricing;
- innovation.

This list, whilst providing a core of skills, will vary from organisation to organisation.

As with other planning functions within a world class organisation, the *business philosophy* must be fully documented to provide a benchmark for performance. The documentation will include a clear statement of vision and intent for each of the elements, the objectives of complete and effective implementation, a full description of the methodology to be employed, the values to be demonstrated together with the accompanying behaviours and practices. Once published, some organisations then incorporate particular sections into other documentation to improve awareness and communication. For instance, the Quicks Group realising that the experience of retail customers visiting a branch was vital to continuing to delight, published the behaviours and practices which affected the internal and external customers directly in a handbook for all employees. It covered a range of activities from dress code to dealing with a customer complaint.

12

Tools for Continuous Improvement

The complete tool box for the team approach to problem-solving and continuous improvement

- **The tools for the systematic approach to continuous improvement**
- **What to use; why to use; when to use; how to use; in simple steps**

INTRODUCTION

Throughout this book there have been references to the use of tools in the continuous improvement process and through learning to use them within the team environment, transferring their use with confidence into the workplace. The most practical tools for use by everyone in the pursuit of world class performance are:

- brainstorming;
- process mapping;
- cause and effect (fishbone) diagrams;
- asking why? – Five times;
- checksheets;
- Pareto analysis;
- matrix analysis;

- consensus-reaching;
- paired comparisons;
- forcefield analysis;
- team purpose analysis;
- Customer–supplier agreements;
- cost–benefit analysis;
- priorities grid;
- time–cost analysis.

There is a galaxy of other, more sophisticated, techniques which are associated with *statistical process control* and *control charting*. They need specialist instruction and interpretation, but are nonetheless important in the march towards world class performance. Once set up, they can be used by virtually anyone as a simple tool of control and monitoring.

BRAINSTORMING

Brainstorming is a technique that encourages creative thinking and the generation of many freewheeling ideas in a short space of time in a team environment.

Sometimes it is difficult to identify what causes a particular process to fail or problem to arise. Rational or conventional thinking does not always reveal the root cause and we continue to solve the same problems over and over again, never really eliminating them. Creative-thinking and approaches to problem-solving often motivate and involve the team and have the potential for providing innovative and alternative answers to problems that have evaded traditional thinking.

Brainstorming should be used when:

- you wish to generate a lot of ideas in a short space of time;
- generating a list of problems;
- identifying possible causes of a problem or process failure;
- identifying possible solutions to a problem;
- developing action plans;
- clarifying a process.

There are some standard rules for brainstorming:

- Appoint one member of the group as a *scribe*;
- The scribe writes down on the flipchart *every* idea and controls the session;
- The scribe asks the closest person for their first idea.
- The idea is written on the flipchart exactly as it is said, with *no modification* or *interpretation* by the scribe.
- The scribe then addresses the next person: there is *no discussion* of the idea at this stage.
- The scribe asks each member of the group in turn going round and round the group in a systematic way until all ideas have been exhausted.
- A member who has no idea this time may *pass*; it may be that other ideas will spark a thought next time round.
- The session ends when the free flow of ideas dries up, i.e. most people are passing or taking a long time to think when it is their turn.

It is only at this stage when the brainstorm has ended that discussion on individual ideas may take place. *For this task all ideas are equally valid.*

FLOWCHARTS OR PROCESS MAPS

Flowcharts are pictures of processes or problems. When examining any process it is necessary to record the series of events and activities, stages and decisions in a form that can be easily understood and communicated to all. Flowcharts can be used at any stage when you wish to determine the flow of work or alternative activities. They are always used at the start of the problem-solving process and are the foundation for continuous improvement. They are used to ensure complete understanding of the process or problem by the whole team and to ensure that the team does have the full range of knowledge required.

Making flowcharts allows graphical representation of the processes and provides information on:

- where the process starts;
- the sequence of events;
- details of the processes and how the steps relate;
- any decisions that are made during the process (and any alternative courses of action that result);
- where the process ends;
- other problems that can be the subject of problem-solving teams later;
- loopholes in the process that are potential sources of trouble;
- where to gather data and on what;
- flowcharts can be applied to any process, from manufacturing, to preparing an invoice, or a training programme, to the steps in making a sale. Because flowcharts will be created and viewed by teams throughout the TQM process, it is vital that they are consistent and that authors use the same symbols in the same way. The symbols in Figure 12.1 have been proven to provide this simplicity and consistency and make communication easier.

The sequence in producing a flowchart is:

- define the boundaries of the process;
- use the simplest symbols possible;
- make sure every feedback loop leads somewhere (*no* dangling boxes);
- there is only one output arrow from a process box and only two from a decision box;
- if there is any doubt as to what happens next, you need an extra member in your team who does know.

Symbol	Description

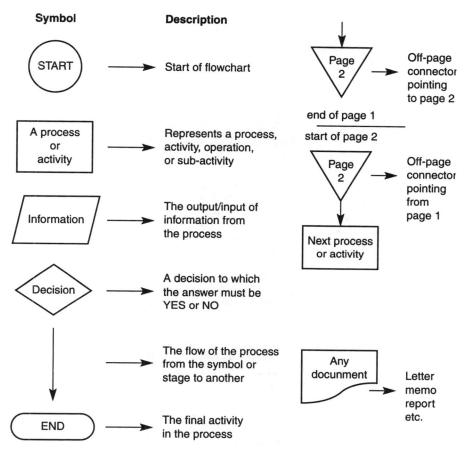

Fig 12.1 Flowchart symbols

Flowcharts and problem-solving

The team must involve the people with the greatest knowledge of the process, the failure or the problem. Together, they draw the flowchart of the existing process as they know it. Any gaps in the knowledge are filled by inviting additional members to the team. A second flowchart is then produced by the team of what should or could be the process. By comparing the two charts, sources of waste, failure or problems can be highlighted and the areas where improvements could be made (Figure 12.2). If a chart becomes too complex, use another sheet.

Flowcharts also provide considerable insight into operational methods, the success of TQM implementation and any potential problems in implementing improvements.

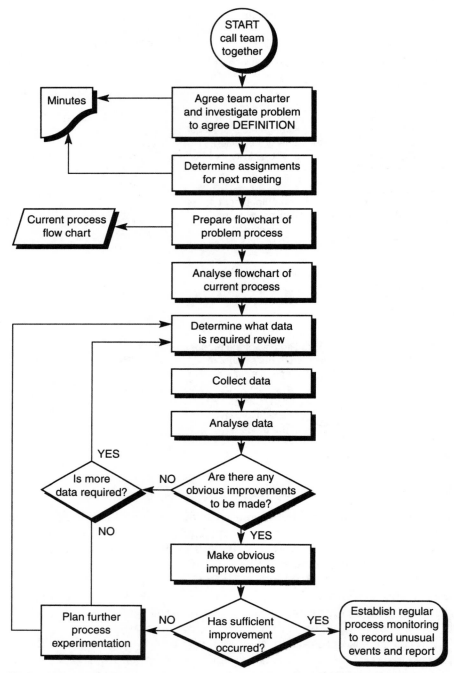

Fig 12.2 Example flowchart: an overview of the process for a problem-solving team

CAUSE AND EFFECT ANALYSIS

Cause and effect analysis uses Ishikawa or fishbone diagrams to help identify the possible causes affecting a failure in a process, a problem or a project. A cause and effect diagram is a simple yet powerful method of visually recording possible causes and relating them to the effects, such as the results of a brainstorm. The Japanese engineer Dr Kaoru Ishikawa (1915–89) emphasised the use of Pareto diagrams and fishbones to prioritise quality improvements.

This tool is used when:

- defining a problem;
- identifying possible data requirements;
- identifying possible causes;
- developing objectives and criteria for solutions;
- narrowing down the problem and the causes;

The way to use this analysis is:

- name the problem in terms of its observable effects;
- identify the *major* categories of *causes* usually things like manpower, materials, methods and machines;
- identify all possible causes using a brainstorm to determine the outline headings and them a separate brainstorm for each of the categories.

Here are some simple rules for success:

- Use large diagrams.
- Involve everyone in the team.
- Examine all relationships, especially the obscure ones. They can often lead you to the true root cause which everyone keeps missing.
- If too many causes are established, review and redefine the *effect*. More than 20 causes and you are beginning to get into trivia.
- Do not get bogged down with problem-solving until you have completed the chart and have the whole picture.
- Double check that you have included everything, you may even wait until the next meeting to have a further brainstorm to ensure all possible causes have been flushed out.

There are several factors to take into account when creating cause and effect diagrams:

- The effect can be a problem, a change or an improvement. The team may want to find out why something is wrong, why something has changed for the worse or why something is so *good*.

- Categories, such as manpower, machine, method and materials are no doubt good for manufacturing, but others will be needed elsewhere. Ishikawa had what he called his five Ps; People, Product, Plant, Process and Programme. These translate into People, Service, Equipment, Systems and Schedules for the service industries. There are many more, you must use what the team believes is appropriate.

- The diagram should have four or five legs, but six or three are quite permissible. Too many means you are likely to be dealing with trivia.

- It is sometimes difficult to be sure of the *cause* categories at the start. Team members may keep quiet because they are unsure into which category their suggestion should be put. In these cases, the leader can run a brainstorm of causes, free from categories altogether. Suggestions can then be gathered under cause headings to help create a proper cause and effect diagram. It can be beneficial to stop and allow ideas to incubate for a short period, until the next team meeting, but no longer than a week.

- Analyse causes and identify links between then (if any). Evaluate the most likely causes (or combinations) and agree to focus on these for root causes and future corrective actions. Remember, if the Pareto rule is applied to the identified causes (or combinations) then 80 per cent of the causes of the observed effect can be eliminated by tackling 20 per cent of the causes.

- After improvements to a process have been made and executed, create another 'fishbone' chart of the outstanding causes, different effects and values will emerge. This will provide pointers for corrective actions in the future. That is the continuous improvement process.

Creating a cause and effect diagram

Having chosen a problem, one of the best ways of narrowing down to the root cause is use of the cause and effect diagram. First of all, the *effect*, the observed problem, is put into a box at the end of the chart (Figure 12.3).

Next, the *cause* headings under which the causes come are added to each leg (Figure 12.4). Use the four Ms or Ishikawa's five Ps or whatever the team decides is appropriate.

Third, if you did not conduct an open brainstorm prior to establishing the cause headings, conduct one for each on the headings in the normal way. Sometimes it may be easier to use separate lists for suggestions under each heading, although it is better to consider the whole list together in the

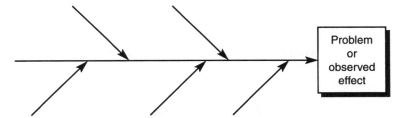

Fig 12.3 First stage in creating a cause and effect diagram

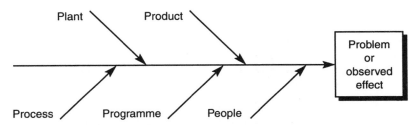

Fig 12.4 Cause headings are added

team and to agree the collapse of some causes into others, each recognising the interdependence of the causes (Figure 12.5).

Finally, ring the most likely causes (Figure 12.6). Rank them in order of importance. If a consensus is not immediately forthcoming, use the technique of 'paired comparisons' sometimes known as the 'Emphasis curve ranking' technique (this is fully described later). It does avoid possible conflict and the problems associated with voting.

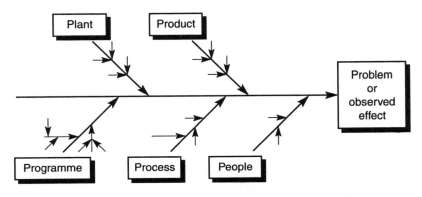

Fig 12.5 Details added to the fishbone under each cause heading

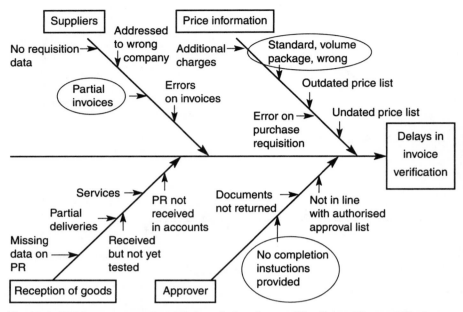

Fig 12.6 Fishbone example of delays in invoice verification with most likely causes ringed

ASKING WHY FIVE TIMES

Asking why is a simple technique used to analyse the apparent causes of problems guiding you towards the root cause when you have little or no hard data. It works as follows:

- Why is the delivery late? *The driver did not arrive on time.*
- Why did the driver not arrive on time? *He overslept.*
- Why did he oversleep? *He was doing too much overtime.*
- Why was he doing too much overtime? *There aren't enough drivers.*
- Why aren't there enough drivers? . . .

The technique enables you to dig deeper than the surface and consequently identify the correct problem on which to concentrate effort. But this is still subjective, we need facts if we are to know the true extent of each *cause*, we need to gather some *data* and analyse it.

DATA COLLECTION AND ANALYSIS

There are many different techniques for gathering information about a process failure, problem, project or solution. In this section we are going to look in detail at two methods of data collection, *checksheets* and *flowcharts*. Then, five methods of analysing the data will be covered to provide pictorial displays. These will enable wider communication and understanding by non-specialists.

The methods described can be used at any appropriate point in the problem solving and continuous improvement process when *facts* and not fiction, or guessing, are required, or when monitoring the solution during and after implementation.

Data represented well visually aids communication and adds impact when presented to individuals or teams. Display helps to highlight data relationships and trends and enables non-specialists to become involved.

Checksheets

Checksheets are a simple and effective way of systematically recording and structuring data. They can be used at any stage in the problem-solving, continuous improvement or monitoring process. The way to use them is as follows:

- First, agree on the exact event or activity to be observed so that everyone involved is tracking the same thing. Decide how to organise the data, by defect, machine, section, employee, shift, etc.

- Decide on the collection period, how often and for how long. The period can be just hours, sometimes days, even weeks or months.

- Design the checksheet in a simple format that will enable you to gather the most information using the least effort. It must be simple to follow, easy to use and large enough to record all the information. Figure 12.7 shows one example and Figure 12.8 a tally chart.

- Take your time in agreeing of what is to be collected. You will not make any friends by going back for more after the exercise has been completed. There are many sources of data all around you, you must decide which source is most appropriate.

- Brief those who are to collect the data, ensure they know what is to be recorded, how and why. Get others committed to complete the task accurately.

- Collect the data, check understanding by follow up, do not trust to luck.

- Always communicate the results to those who have been involved, when they have been analysed.

Reasons	1991 Nov	1991 Dec	1992 Jan	1992 Feb	Total
Returned goods	31	26	26	21	104
Errors in pricing	18	20	20	10	68
Short delivery	5	1	3	2	11
Passed late from departments	4	2	4		10
Incorrect address	2	2	1	1	6
Late from supplier		1	2		3
Wrong goods sent in first place				1	1
Holidays		1			1
TOTAL	60	53	56	35	204

Fig 12.7 Example checksheet on reasons for delays in invoice payment

Mistakes		March		Total
	1	2	3	
Centring	II	III	III	8
Spelling	IIII II	IIII IIII I	IIII	23
Punctuation	IIII IIII IIII	IIII IIII	IIII IIII IIII	40
Missed paragraphs	II	I	I	4
Wrong numbers	III	IIII	III	10
Wrong page numbers	I	I	II	4
Tables	IIII	IIII	IIII	13
TOTAL	34	35	33	102

Fig 12.8 Example tally chart on typing mistakes

Data analysis and display

There are many ways of displaying the data collected, such as Pareto diagrams, line graphs, pie charts, histograms, frequency distributions and scatter graphs. However, here we will deal with just Pareto analysis. We have already seen a further method of display, this time during collection, the *tally chart*, (Figure 12.8). Examples of other forms of data display are given at the end of this chapter.

Pareto analysis (the 80/20 rule)

This is a simple method that helps separate major causes of the problem from the minor ones, displayed in the form of a ranked vertical bar chart. This method is often known as the 80/20 rule, sorting the *vital few* from the *trivial many*. Vilfredo Pareto (1848–1923) was an Italian economist who spent many years studying the distribution of wealth. His findings pointed to the fact that a majority of wealth went to a minority of people, in most instances. M O Lorenz put the Pareto concepts into graphical form as Pareto charts, showing the distribution of wealth by the various categories. Recently, these concepts have been applied to the approach used to prioritise decision-making, because the main causes of a problem can often be shown up as just a few items which will stand out from a long list of unimportant items. For instance, it can be shown that in a warehouse, 80 per cent of the company's business is done on 20 per cent of the lines it has in stock. Plotting onto a Pareto chart enables the team to decide where the major contributory categories of a problem occur and consequently where they should place their efforts when looking for solutions to that problem. The Pareto chart is a column graph ranked in priority sequence in descending order. A cumulative line is often added to the chart so that changes can be more readily monitored. It also shows the percentage a particular category, or categories added together, representative of the total problem. A Pareto diagram can also be used to show the difference between 'before' and 'after' . The diagrams are drawn in the following way:

- Decide which data is to be charted.
- Decide how the data is to be classified.
- Collect data for a specified time period.
- Arrange the data in descending order.
- Convert to percentage (if required) using the other side of the graph to show percentages.
- Plot the results on a diagram.

- Plot 'cumulative' line.
- Record 'key' and source of data.
- Plot improvement columns and new 'cumulative' line.

Figure 12.9 shows the largest numbers of errors are caused by 'Wrong addresses' and 'Wrong descriptions', but when costs are added the order of importance changes (Figure 12.10).

The conclusion here is that 80 per cent of the costs of invoice problems can be found in four of the various reasons. However, we also know that 82 per cent of the problems are to be found in three of the problem categories, only one of which appears in the 80 per cent of the cost of the problem. This provides objective information on which to base the decision as which problem to tackle first (Figure 12.11).

Problem	No.
Wrong address	400
Wrong description	300
Late postage	120
Wrong prices	50
Bad addition	30
Others	100
Total	1,000

Fig 12.9 Most errors are caused by wrong addresses or descriptions

Problem	No.	Cost each £	Total cost £	Order
Wrong address	400	2.50	1000	4
Wrong description	300	3.00	900	5
Late postage	120	10.00	1200	3
Wrong prices	50	80.00	4000	1
Bad addition	30	60.00	1800	2
Others	100	11.00	1100	
Total	1,000		10,000	

Fig 12.10 Relating cost of errors changes scale of problem

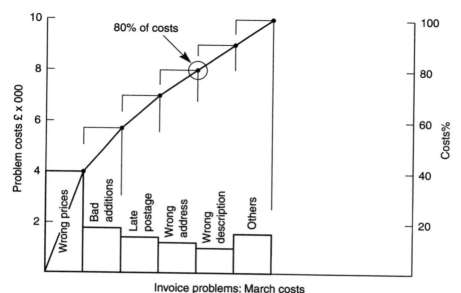

Fig 12.11 **Pareto diagram with cumulative line provides objective information on which to base priorities**

MATRIX ANALYSIS

This is useful when trying to prioritise from a list of problems, or when trying to give some structure to a large quantity of varying data. The method of use is as follows:

- List all of the problems or data sets under consideration.
- Choose criteria for evaluation. For example; is the problem worthwhile?; is there management support?; can it be done?; is the cost high or low?; is the timescale short, medium or long-term?
- Each person in the team fills in a pre-prepared matrix, and the results are summarised to arrive at the decision as in Figure 12.12

CONSENSUS REACHING

Making decisions is an important aspect of any manager's job and possibly the most difficult problem to tackle. Involving those who are affected by a decision will contribute to making the right decision. *Consensus reaching*

Problem	Worthwhile	Mgmt. support	Do-able	Cost	Time scale
1	5 yes 2 no	Y	6 yes 1 no	High	Short
2	5 yes 2 no	Y	3 yes 3 no	High	Med
3	3 yes 4 no	N	1 yes 5 no	High	Med
4	4 yes 3 no	N	3 yes 4 no	Low	Short
5	6 yes 1 no	Y	7 yes 0 no	?	Long

Fig 12.12 A simple matrix analysis

enables a group of people to arrive at an agreed decision in a structured way. The method is as follows:

- *Explain the need for a decision* Review the circumstances leading to the need to make a decision. Ensure that everyone understands the need.
- *Brainstorm ideas and alternatives* Using brainstorm rules, log ideas/solutions/alternatives.
- *Check on understanding* Ensure that all contributions are fully understood by all present.
- *Determine the number of votes* Give a reasonable number of votes to each member of the group (fewer votes than ideas: ten ideas, five votes). Agree the maximum number of votes a member can give to any one idea.
- *Allocate votes* Ask each member to allocate votes to their preferred solution(s). Select the solution(s) with the most votes. If necessary, go to round two, allocating votes only to the selected solution(s). Voting tests opinion. It does not in itself secure consensus.
- *Check for practicality* Review the results. Check that the solution(s) is feasible and that other solutions are less appropriate.
- *Ask for consensus* Ask each member to agree to the selected solution.

This approach enables each member in the group to:

- contribute actively to the decision;
- gain a clear understanding of another's point of view.

With the result that the elected viewpoint will have a high degree of acceptance and commitment from everyone.

Remember that majority agreement is *not* consensus. Everyone has to accept the way forward.

PAIRED COMPARISONS OR EMPHASIS CURVE RANKING

In many situations several options will be available. A number of critical areas for improvement will be agreed on the face of things of equal importance, but there is still a need to determine which option or combination of options provides the best way forward. Paired selection enables each member to systematically analyse a list of ideas or problems, goals or anything really, against agreed criteria and priorities, and it avoids the problems associated with voting. It uses a diagram similar to that in Figure 12.13.

Each member of the team with a comparison chart and list will individually:

- List all the contending items on the left.
- Determine the evaluation criteria, i.e. the questions you are going to use to evaluate the pairs of options, e.g. which is more benefit in short term? Which is most likely to have success?

No.	Item	Total					
1			1 2	1 3	1 4	1 5	1 6
2			2 3	2 4	2 5	2 6	
3			3 4	3 5	3 6		
4			4 5	4 6			
5			5 6				
6							

Fig 12.13 Emphasis curve ranking table

- Compare the first two items and decide which is the more important. The choice will be ringed in column 1, row 1.

- The problem is repeated, comparing item 1 with item 3, item 1 with item 4 and so on until finally, item 5 is compared with item 6. Each time, the choice is ringed in the appropriate column and row.

- When all have been ringed, the ringed 1's are counted and the total written against item 1 in the total column. This is repeated for the ringed 2's and so on for the other numbers.

The team leader then totals the team members' allocated scores against each item using a vote matrix ranking table similar to Figure 12.14. Once completed, the list is rewritten in order of computed rank.

Paired comparisons or emphasis curve technique enables priorities to be agreed in a quick and qualitative manner using agreed criteria. It is helpful in deciding priorities when a number of options are available, all of which seem equally important.

FORCE FIELD ANALYSIS

Force field analysis (FFA) is a technique for identifying the forces that help or obstruct a change you want to make. It is used to:

- improve any situation that requires change;

- understand what is working for and against any proposal you wish to make;

- identify forces which cannot be changed in order to make contingency plans.

Item	Team members' votes	Total	Ranking
1			
2			
3			
4			
5			
6			

Fig 12.14 Vote matrix ranking table

It is used whenever you want to change the way of doing something or are planning to overcome barriers to change. It is used as follows:

- Select a problem. Describe the problem as you see it at the moment.
- A problem statement is written describing first, the present situation and second, the situation as you would like it.
- It is likely that there are some forces pushing in the direction you want to go and others resisting . This situation can be shown as in Figure 12.15.

List as many forces as you can, trying to really probe the situation. It may call for a brainstorm.

- Consider your list, and decide which forces you can do something about. Highlight these in some way.
- For each *resisting force* highlighted, brainstorm as many action steps as you can which you might be able to plan and carry out to reduce the effect of the force or eliminate it completely.
- Examine each *driving force* highlighted and list all the action steps which would increase the effect of each driving force.

You are trying to encourage the positive forces and discourage the negative ones.

Use the template in Figure 12.16 to build up your diagram. When applied to a real example, the result can appear similar to Figure 12.17.

Each *driving* factor identified should provide a list of action steps to increase the effect. Each *resisting* factor should be brainstormed to provide as many action steps as possible to reduce the effects or eliminate it completely. Finally, if the problem is complex, a matrix can be used to consider your ability to influence the various factors taken from a force

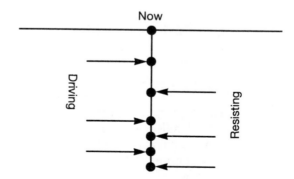

Fig 12.15 Force field outline

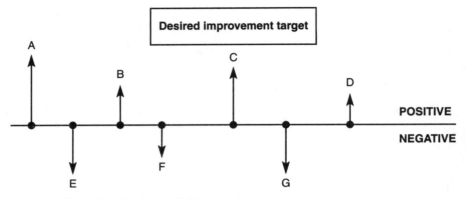

Fig 12.16 Template for force field analysis

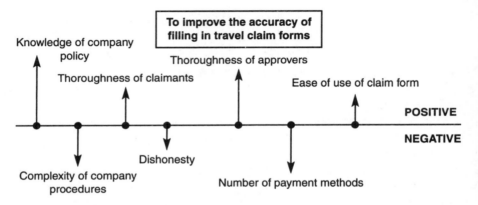

Fig 12.17 Example of force field analysis

field analysis sheet (Figure 12.18). You can then identify the restraining forces which are to be tackled and develop an action plan.

Force field analysis provides a disciplined and systematic approach to harnessing common sense. It is particularly useful when planning to initiate change.

We all know that pushing to open at a shut door is a lot easier if we release the catch first. We will still have to push, but the force we use has more effect if we reduce the restraint. It is the same with the implementation of change. There comes a point where there is no more effort that can be brought to bear and you must reduce some of the restraints. However, to do that you need to identify them.

Positive forces				Negative forces			
Force	Ability to influence	Effect	Total	Force	Ability to influence	Effect	Total
Knowledge of company policy	5	6	11	Complexity of company procedure	1	4	5
Thoroughness of claimants	3	6	9	Number of payments methods	4	1	5
Thoroughness of approvers	2	3	5				
Ease of use of claim form	8	6	14				
Forces which cannot be influenced: Dishonesty							

Fig 12.18 Force field analysis sheet

TEAM PURPOSE ANALYSIS

This is a process which helps a team or unit:

- define its purpose and align with the business strategy and goals *and in that way is one of the prime methods used for mission and goal deployment into the organisation, down the management line to the individual;*
- define the requirements, measurements and working relationship with its customers and suppliers;
- carry out an activity/task analysis to show what is currently being done and why;
- identify whether or not each activity meets specific customer requirements and is right first time;
- make immediate gains;
- identify improvement projects for action.

There are five main stages:

- What is our role?
  - What do we think we do?
  - What skills/talent do we have?
- Does this line up with the business mission/goals/objectives?
  - Is there an obvious 'fit'?
  - Does our manager agree?

- Who are our customers and suppliers?
  - What are their requirements?
  - How should we measure our/their performance?
- What do we actually do?
  - How do we spend our time and resources?
  - What are the processes for meeting our customer's requirements?
  - Are all of our activities required?
  - How much of our activity meets customer requirements and is right first time?
  - What waste and failure do we generate?
  - How much effort goes into inspection and correction?
  - What are the opportunities for improvement?
- What do we need to do to improve?
  - Check activities against mission, goals, customer requirements.
  - Prioritise improvement opportunities.
  - Identify projects.
  - Implement projects using PDCA.
  - Identify and display key measures.
  - Monitor and review progress.

Team purpose analysis helps a team focus its activities on the needs of its customers. It also ensures first, that waste is identified and second that the team's activities are aligned to business goals/objectives. Figure 12.19 shows its use in the initial goals cascade and Figure 12.20 (on page 186) shows a typical flowchart.

CUSTOMER–SUPPLIER AGREEMENTS

A customer–supplier agreement (CSA) is a written document which specifies the needs of a customer (both internal and external), what the supplier can deliver and what is to be done in case of changed circumstances. In some companies it is called a 'service level agreement'. The sequence of events is as follows:

- *Decide on key customer–supplier relationship* The two main players – the supplier of the output and the customer, should agree in principle that a written agreement would improve the quality chain.
- *Identify all interested parties* Make sure that all interested parties understand what is involved and are willing to 'buy in' to the agreement.
- *Generate a draft document* The two main players should informally discuss their customer–supplier relationship and generate a draft document

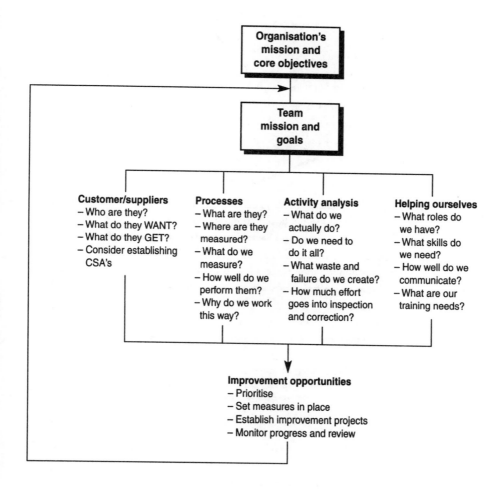

Fig 12.19 Use of team purpose analysis in the initial goals cascade

which spells out their agreement(s). A CSA checklist is shown as part of Figure 12.21 (on page 187). Aim to keep the draft as simple as possible.

- *Agreement discussion* The main players and other interested parties should meet – any additions to the agreement are added at this stage.
- *Agreement in principle* Main players (or their representatives) and interested parties etc, sign the draft agreement.

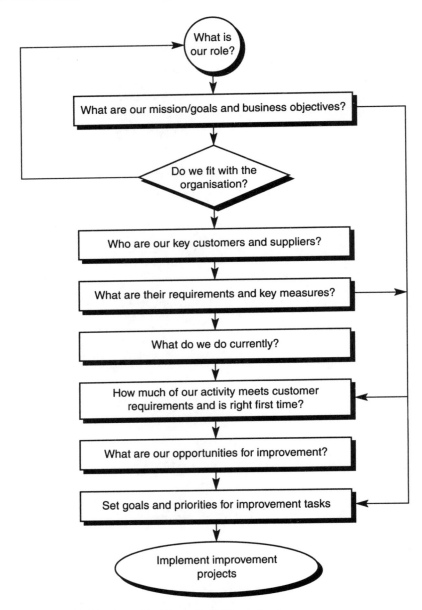

Fig 12.20 Typical team purpose analysis flowchart

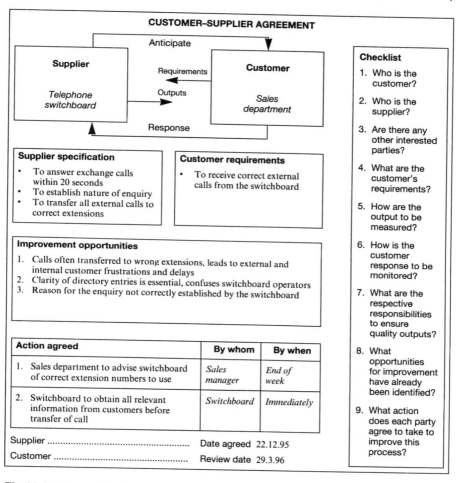

CUSTOMER–SUPPLIER AGREEMENT

Supplier		Customer
Supplier	Anticipate	**Customer**
Telephone switchboard	Requirements / Outputs / Response	Sales department

Supplier specification

- To answer exchange calls within 20 seconds
- To establish nature of enquiry
- To transfer all external calls to correct extensions

Customer requirements

- To receive correct external calls from the switchboard

Improvement opportunities

1. Calls often transferred to wrong extensions, leads to external and internal customer frustrations and delays
2. Clarity of directory entries is essential, confuses switchboard operators
3. Reason for the enquiry not correctly established by the switchboard

Action agreed	By whom	By when
1. Sales department to advise switchboard of correct extension numbers to use	Sales manager	End of week
2. Switchboard to obtain all relevant information from customers before transfer of call	Switchboard	Immediately

Supplier .... Date agreed 22.12.95

Customer .... Review date 29.3.96

Checklist

1. Who is the customer?
2. Who is the supplier?
3. Are there any other interested parties?
4. What are the customer's requirements?
5. How are the output to be measured?
6. How is the customer response to be monitored?
7. What are the respective responsibilities to ensure quality outputs?
8. What opportunities for improvement have already been identified?
9. What action does each party agree to take to improve this process?

Fig 12.21 Example of agreement between customer and supplier

- *Trial period* The agreement is for a trial period and amended as required at the end of the period.
- *Regular review* The CSA is reviewed regularly as agreed between main players.

A CSA can help ensure that the expectations of customer and supplier are similar and highlight the element which are key to maintaining a quality output. It fosters teamwork between different departments. They can become complicated – often it is best to start with a letter of understanding and add to it as problems are exposed. The approach can also be used informally with equally good results in terms of starting the process of understanding the interdependence of customer and supplier and self measurement.

COST–BENEFIT ANALYSIS

Cost–benefit analysis is a technique for comparing the costs of taking a particular course of action with the benefits achievable from the outcome. It is a method of assessing the viability of the course of action in monetary terms. Technique:

- Decide on the period over which the analysis will be performed.
- Identify all of the factors involved which will incur costs or provide benefits. Brainstorming can be used at this stage.
- Separate the factors into those that incur cost and those that produce monetary benefit. Be sure to identify hidden costs such as parallel running, maintenance, additional training and so on.
- Assess each of the factors and estimate a monetary value.
- Add the total costs and the total benefits.

Fig 12.22 shows an example.

Often you would use this technique to compare solutions in conjunction with evaluating the non-financial benefits.

PRIORITIES GRID

A priorities grid is a tool to help a team decide which option or solution to adopt using the criteria of pay-off and ease of implementation. Method as follows:

- Brainstorm the options.
- Assess the payoff available for each option (if it helps, do a full cost–benefit analysis). Rate each option on a scale from one to six; six being the biggest pay-off.
- Assess the ease of implementation of each option in terms of time, resources, knock-on effects and rate each one from one to six; six being the easiest to implement.
- Build up a grid to show the relative positions of the options against the two scales. Use Post-It notes to do this so that you can easily move the

Costs (£)	Year					Total
	1	2	3	4	5	
Purchase of equipment	1,000	–	–	–	–	1,000
Less trade in	200	–	–	–	–	200
Net purchase price	800	–	–	–	–	800
Maintenance contract	–	150	150	150	150	600
Training	400	100	100	100	100	800
Software	500	–	–	200	–	700
Total costs	1,700	250	250	450	250	2,900

Benefits (£)	Year					Total
	1	2	3	4	5	
Staff savings	2,000	2,700	2,700	2,700	2,700	12,800
Reduced consumables	400	800	800	800	800	3,600
Total benefits	2,400	3,500	3,500	3,500	3,500	16,400

Analysis

Benefit to cost ratio

$$= \frac{\text{value of benefits}}{\text{total costs}} = \frac{16,400}{2,900} = 5.6:1$$

Net annual benefit

$$= \text{Annual benefit} - \text{Annual cost}$$
$$= 2,400 - 1,700 = 700$$

Net annual benefit
(average of all years)

$$= \frac{\text{Total benefits} - \text{Total costs}}{5}$$

$$= \frac{16,400 - 2,900}{5} = £2,700$$

Fig 12.22 Example of cost–benefit analysis for buying a computer

options around on the grid until you are happy they are in the correct relative positions.

- Clearly, the nearer the top right hand corner of the grid, the better the option. Use the relative positions of all the options to decide which will give the greatest payoff while being easy to do.

The priorities grid (Figure 12.23) is a quick and simple tool for differentiating between a range of potential solutions.

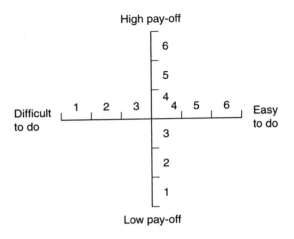

Fig 12.23 Priorities grid

TIME–COST ANALYSIS

Time–cost analysis is a graphical way of illustrating the relationship between the time taken to complete stages of a process; the amount of cost-added or invested in each stage and the overall cycle time. The sequence is:

- Identify the process or sub-process to be analysed.
- Identify the specific steps that make up the process.
- Collect data on:
  - amount of time spent at each stage;
  - amount of cost added at each stage;
  - the total cycle time.

If there is significant variation in the process, use control charts to identify the mean.

- Plot cost added against time for each step of the process.
- Use this graph to question:
  - areas of high investment of time;
  - areas of high cost added;
  - within time bands, amount of active as opposed to waiting time as a basis for identifying process improvements.

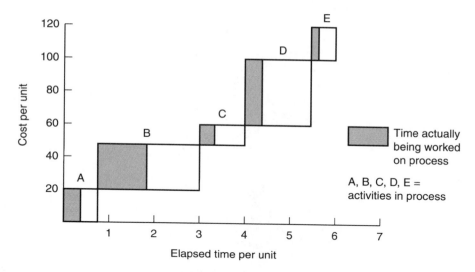

Fig 12.24 Example of time–cost analysis

The goal of the analysis is to:

- reduce cycle time;
- increase added value more quickly;
- remove non-value steps.

Time–cost analysis can be used to identify the areas of greatest cost (in terms of time and money) as a starting point for process improvement (Figure 12.24).

FURTHER EXAMPLES OF DATA DISPLAY

Frequency histogram

Displays the frequency distribution over a range of values. The addition of a 3D effect can further enhance the display (Figure 12.25 overleaf). Main uses are:

- to highlight a particular problem;
- to assess performance to a given standard;
- specification, tolerance, degree of allowable non-conformance.

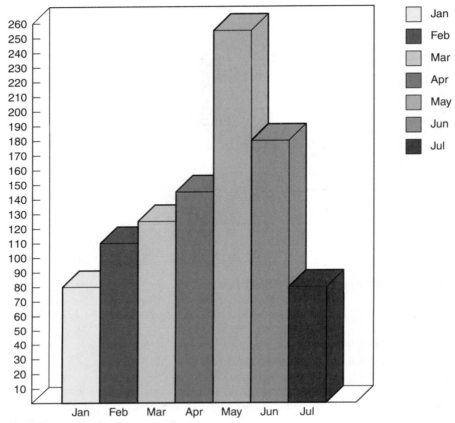

Fig 12.25 Frequency histogram

Line graph

Displays a direct relationship between two variables (Figure 12.26).

Pie chart

Displays a complete set of data and the proportions (if required) represented by each 'slice' of the whole at any point in time (Figure 12.27). Pie charts can be used to: emphasise a particular segment and show a full picture of total components.

Frequency distribution

When using this method, tally results produce a bell shaped curve of the normal distribution, displaying the *average* values together with the *range*

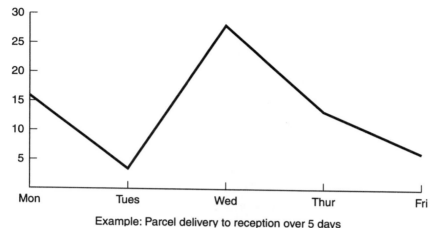

Example: Parcel delivery to reception over 5 days

Fig 12.26 Line graph

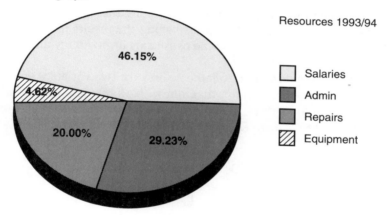

Resources 1993/94

- Salaries
- Admin
- Repairs
- Equipment

Fig 12.27 Pie chart

or *spread* (Figure 12.28 overleaf). The normal measure of the *average* is known as the *mean*. The mean is calculated by adding all the values together and dividing by the number of values. This gives a summary measure of the central point of the data.

Two other measures of the average are the *median* and the *mode*. The median is the middle value when the values are arranged in ascending or descending order. The mode is the most commonly-occurring value in the set of data. The simplest measure of the *spread* is the *range* between the highest and the lowest value. The most important value of spread or dispersion is the *standard deviation*. Standard deviation is the average difference between the values and the mean.

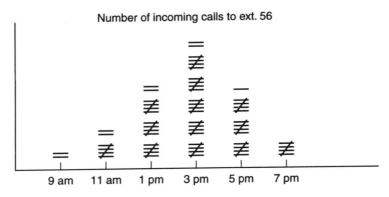

Fig 12.28 **Bell-shaped normal distribution curve**

Scatter diagrams

The scatter diagram is a method of determining the relationships between *cause* and *effect* patterns and then displaying the results in an easily read graphical form. It is best to draw the cause axis horizontally and the effect axis vertically.

Correlation is the term used to indicate how the two variables are related. After you have drawn the scatter diagram with all the data points inserted, see if it is possible to draw a straight line to represent the relationship between the two variables. This is called the *best fit line*, but is not always possible (Figure 12.29).

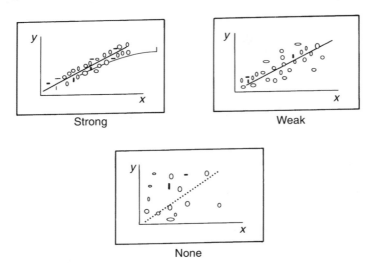

Fig 12.29 **Scatter diagrams with best-fit lines**

13

Establishing Supplier Partnerships

Being customer-focused also means being supplier-focused; establishing standards with your supppliers and continuous assessment is the only way to ensure quality inputs to your processes.

- A total quality approach to assessing suppliers
- Establishing the second party audit culture
- Continuous monitoring and assessment

INTRODUCTION

Once you have gained control of your own processes by implementing internal culture changes, process management-orientation, teamwork for process improvement and all the other initiators and sustainers of moving towards world class performance, you will be in a position to start work on improving the quality of your inputs from external sources.

There are many common sayings about working with sub-standard materials and services, '... you cannot make a silk purse out of a sows ear,' and more recently in computer terminology 'garbage in means garbage out'. So if you really want to make a permanent improvement to the quality of your outputs you must improve the quality of your inputs. World class organisations influence their suppliers' attitudes towards the quality of their product and service. They do this by developing a partnership with them, treating them as customers, identifying their requirements and making performance improvement agreements tied to continuing business. They measure supplier performance very tightly, monitoring not just product or service quality in terms of meeting requirements right first time on time, but through careful and regular physical assessment.

As an organisation wishing to become world class, you will almost certainly need to develop a system by which to measure supplier performance and provide a quantitative as well as a qualitative rating for them.

By developing a partnership with your suppliers through customer–supplier agreements, you can influence your quality by improving supplier quality and the quality of interaction between you. Then you will need to implement both a system for measuring performance and for assessment through on-site inspection and audit, called second party audit. With the 1994 update and revision of ISO 9000 there is an implied need to work more closely with suppliers for continuous improvement and prevention.

SUPPLIER ASSESSMENT: PARTNERSHIP IN IMPROVING QUALITY

A supplier assessment is what is termed a *second party audit*, by you, or someone acting on your behalf, on your supplier. It is an audit against *your requirements* and *specifications*. As with third party audits (audits by a third party, not associated with you against an independent set of requirements and specifications), they are both types of *external audit* as opposed to the first party audit which is internal – *us on us*.

Second party audits carried out by one company on another are those which originally came along with the idea of quality assurance where a major purchaser would audit its suppliers. There are a number of reasons why a company may wish to audit its suppliers:

- world class performance demands it;
- ISO 9000 implies a need for it;
- provides an input into selecting, grading and improving suppliers;
- provides help to improve the quality systems of suppliers;
- increases mutual understanding of quality requirements;
- leads to 'supply chain tuning' towards, JIT, TQM, etc.

There may be other reasons and from an ideal point of view, it is accepted that if audits are only done for the first two reasons above, then they will not be of the greatest value. However, they remain the only reasons for some companies. Many major purchasers carry out supplier audits to advise user departments of areas of weakness in suppliers so that appropriate contract or surveillance mechanisms can be instigated if the supplier is given work. It can also highlight the additional costs likely.

A second party system of auditing can be programmed over a long term, as with internal quality system audits, if the auditor company has a fairly stable list of suppliers it has approved for use.

Suppliers are constantly seeking new markets and customers and those customers demand different methods and systems. Such changes may have a knock-on effect to existing customers, effects that can be both beneficial and detrimental. Potential customers are being bombarded by potential suppliers and where it appears there is a commercial benefit in opening up a new source of supply, the customer may wish to audit that potential supplier. In a competitive bidding situation, a company may wish to audit all bidders as an input to the ultimate purchase decision. Having made that decision, the company may wish to carry out surveillance audits to ensure contract requirements are fully understood and are being met, especially after changes to contract requirements.

The results of all these visits and audits combine to form a grading and perhaps also a performance rating into which are combined other relevant quality features such as price, delivery, results of inspection of received lots, service, communication, etc. Those suppliers that have gained a high or best rating, might deserve some commercial advantage if it is considered that audits and inspections of their operations can be reduced or minimised as a result of their proven performance.

The planning of the audits and the review system is vital to successful co-operation with suppliers, and they must be aware, involved and contribute to it so that it is viewed as a desirable part of the collaboration between two organisations.

Often a company which understands that it cannot inspect quality into its own products and services, tries to inspect quality into suppliers' systems. This manifests itself as a 'policeman' approach by the auditor, who arrives with minimum announcement, determined to 'get' the supplier with a few operating and system discrepancies. The aim should be to help the supplier to identify problems, by acting as a fresh pair of outside eyes, and prepared to offer advice in their solution. The penalty-issuing auditor will create the desire to cover up rather than expose difficulties it may be encountering. If exposure results in help and advice being offered rather than business being withdrawn, then clearly it will foster a partnership and will assist in the development of a strength which is resistant to outside forces. The principles behind this are not new, but they are not often practised. Being rude to, irritating or simply bullying suppliers, whether internal or external, guarantees that you will achieve one thing – conflict. A firm hand is required, but it must be used to lead and support rather than to beat the supplier into submission.

Any supplier quality audit and review system should be designed to assess suppliers through a complete survey of their producing systems. The objective should be to improve the four Cs: *communication, capability, confidence* and *control*. This will develop respect for each party and make sure that the frequency and organisation of the audits is appropriate (Figure 13.1). As with so much in quality assurance management, data will provide the objective evidence of supplier capability. The records must be used with skill and sensitivity to forge long-term associations, building trust and collaboration for continuity and mutual success.

The prime objective of any supplier assessment process must be to assist those suppliers to improve their ability to produce products and services that conform to your changing requirements. Your suppliers' quality is controlled at their points of operation and if they cannot provide the quality you require as an input to your processes, you cannot produce the consistent outputs that your customers require.

It is a case of:

Garbage in: Garbage out

Few companies, even in this age of enlightenment, decide to buy from another company on the basis of a quality audit alone. Many purchasers place orders despite, rather than because of, the results of the quality audits on suppliers.

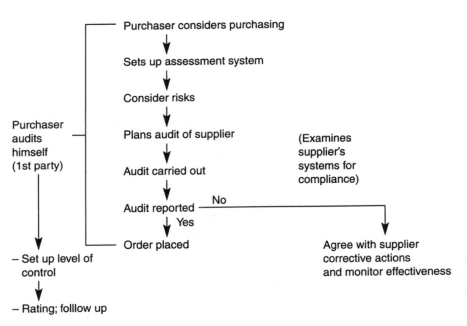

Fig 13.1 The process of supplier (second party) audit

ASSESSMENT

Purchasers must consider how much assurance it is necessary to gain for a particular product or service. A number of aspects will need consideration:

- degree of standardisation;
- quality history;
- ease of inspection of the product, process or service;
- complexity and/or uniqueness;
- consequences of failure;
- special process controls ... etc.

On the basis of these considerations and other similar factors, a decision can be reached as to the relative importance of the supplier having a fully-compliant system and thereby the degree of audit required. This should mean that even if a supplier had a very attractive price and delivery he would not be given a contract to supply where great risk was to be involved because of weaknesses in his quality systems. The converse is also true; it should be the case that suppliers with good and proven quality assurance systems should gain commercial advantage over competitors. Most typically, the situations revealed from audits are of some intermediate state. Purchasers then write into their contracts requirements designed to cater for the 'weakness' highlighted – possibly inspection or surveillance at the point where work is carried out (Figure 13.2 overleaf).

The second party situation outlined is very typical of the way that quality assurance began to be introduced to the supply chain. Auditors representing the major purchasers were seen as very powerful by many of the (smaller) companies audited. If suppliers did not comply with requirements, they could lose business. From this developed the need for a strict code of ethics practised by the auditors. The growth of supplier (or second party) audits demanded a more standardised approach and the purchasing sections of ISO 9000 were designed to cater for this.

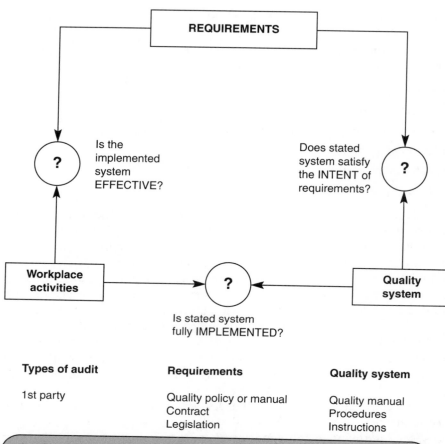

Types of audit	Requirements	Quality system
1st party	Quality policy or manual Contract Legislation	Quality manual Procedures Instructions
2nd Party	Product conditions Service conditions Contract conditions Purchase conditions Quality standard	Quality manual Procedures Specifications and quality plans
3rd party	Quality standard	As 1st party

Fig 13.2 Audit perspectives

14

Working to the Best Standards

Do ISO 9000 and the Investors In People standards have a role in a world class organisation?

- ISO 9000 and IIP are recipes for consistency
- The common building blocks
- A structure for a quality management system
- Is ISO 9000 and the world class organisation model compatible?

INTRODUCTION

It seems to be stating the obvious to say that world class companies work to the best standards; it may be more correct to say that they *operate the best* standards, for they often are the trailblazers that the world's best standards are based up on.

Why is it that MacDonalds can provide the same experience in Derby, Central London, Avignon, Moscow and Palm Beach? How can Walt Disney provide the same experience seven days a week, week in, week out at their theme parks? What is the secret of a Mars bar that wherever it is manufactured it tastes the same?

The answer is very simple. They have reproducible processes and a reproducible culture. In reality, they use the same mechanism as a chef uses to ensure that a 'special' dish tastes the same every time it is ordered and cooked.

The *Concise Oxford English Dictionary* defines recipe as:

'statement of ingredients and procedure for preparing a dish, etc.; device for effecting something consistently'

Consistency is also something we are seeking for a world class organisation, is it not?

So far in this book we have stressed the need to develop process maps which describe the processes of the organisation and to define them in a way that ensures that the outputs of the processes will always meet the customer's requirements. It is just a small step from here to creating *the recipes for success* by adding any necessary specifications (the ingredients such as material specifications, timing, copies to whom and, skill requirements). To do this, not only must the process map be agreed by those who carry it out but any options must be investigated to remove all chance of error and a single method be agreed also, by all.

The process map must be analysed to remove all false customers, to streamline areas where bottlenecks occur, and parts where special or additional training is required identified and action taken. Feedback loops have to be inserted to enable response to the *voice of the process* and the *voice of the customer* to be heard and addressed, to enable the process to continue to meet the needs of the customer even after they have changed their requirements. To the agreed process map should be added the specifications *agreed by all*.

What we have just described is a *quality management system*. This would go a long way to meeting the requirements of the *best standard* for quality management systems, ISO 9000.

You cannot have a quality management system that will meet the requirements of ISO 9000, and continue to do so, without a mass of bureaucracy, without a commitment to total quality management. This is especially so since the changes introduced in July 1994 (ISO 9000:1994) – and you cannot achieve truly world class performance without a quality management system that is well ahead of the requirements of ISO 9000.

This need to commit to the philosophies of total quality has always been part of the ISO 9000 standard, but has, never been part of the audited areas. It has been buried in the supporting documents to be read by the few. Now, in the latest revision, some of it has been brought into the light of day and included in the audited requirements. Let us hope it is not too late to revive what has always been a laudable objective, to achieve the international standard. However, in the absence of the spirit of total quality management the standard has been brought to a sad level of disrepute in the eyes of many because it provides a standard that has permitted mediocrity to be accredited for its consistency.

Any organisation with its sights set on achieving world class status will not be content with just getting by with the regular surveillance visits of external bodies who assess the maintenance of the quality management system as continuing to meet the requirements of the *best standard*.

A short study of the International Standard for Quality Assurance Systems and the National Standard for Investors In People shows many close similarities and common requirements in several principle areas.

These are also common in total quality management theory and in the world class model introduced in chapter 1.

You may be asking *why* is this? The answer is simply that they are all based the same fundamental building blocks of:

- recognising the internal customer–supplier chain;
- the need to focus on a process-oriented structure rather than a functional structure;
- goal-driven measurement of process effectiveness;
- clear leadership and direction;
- good communication up, down and across the organisation;
- a training culture;
- co-ordinated and continuous improvement;
- goal and measurement-based appraisal of individual performance.

HOW DOES ISO 9000 HELP?

If we standardise the key processes of the business and create a recipe for their successful operation which eliminates the assignable variation as far as possible, we will in effect be developing a quality management system. If we are truly committed to developing a world class organisation, we will be measuring our performance at process and individual level and using the results to continuously improve the performance of our processes.

If we wish to monitor that this is really happening throughout the organisation we may carry out cross-functional operational audits. This may satisfy the management of the organisation, but it does not demonstrate to the external customer that the good words on a quality system approach to continuous improvement have been implemented and is effective. Indeed, the external customer might be invited to (and may even insist on) carrying out their own audit, a *second party audit*, to satisfy themselves that the described intent have been implemented effectively in the areas of interest to them. But even this will be of little use in attracting potential and new customers. Much better, a *third party audit* in which an independent body of assessors carries out an audit of the entire quality management system leading to international recognition as having and maintaining a good system, one which meets the requirements of the international standard. The best standard for a quality management system is ISO 9000 even with the shortcomings outlined earlier. It is international and it is being stiffened with regard to the demonstration of some of the environment-creating activities which lead to a total quality culture.

Quality assurance systems based on the ideals of Deming, Juran and Philip Crosby can be traced back to the early 1970s. Yet quality assurance standards can be traced back to the Babylonian Empire when they related to the erection of dwellings. In more recent times, government-sponsored quality assurance standards can be found in use during the Second World War, when they were used to vet manufacturers bidding for government contracts for armaments and other defence requirements. Before a contract was awarded, potential suppliers were 'audited' against a set of standards for *good management practice*, to ensure that the organisation was worthy of being granted the contract. Following the end of the war, these standards found their way into regular use by the Ministry of Defence (DEF STAN) and by NATO which has the AQAP standards, used regularly during the awarding of contracts.

During the early 1970s, the Society of Motor Manufacturers and Traders lobbied hard for the establishment of standards that were more in keeping with the production and supply of non-defence equipment. This led to the establishment in 1975 of BS 5179, which was a guide and non-mandatory. It was used by motor manufacturers extensively in the placement of subcontract work and to improve the quality of their component supply. This in itself led to the establishment of regular second party supplier auditing and assessment.

A standard for the establishment of quality management systems was first published in this country in 1979 by the British Standards Institution, we know it as BS 5750. Several other countries established their own quality management systems standards around the same time. In 1987, these were harmonised by the International Standards Organisation into a common standard which we know as ISO 9000 based on BS 5750. In 1994, further changes were made to the standard (continuous improvement) which have resulted in all national terminology being discarded in favour of the internationally-recognised name ISO 9000. In this country we now refer to the standard as BS EN ISO 9000. (The EN stands for *European Normalisation*. It is also recognised by the European Union.)

Having a quality management system which meets the requirements of the international standard ISO 9000 has three major benefits:

- It provides existing and potential new customers with confidence that the organisation is capable of consistently meeting their requirements now and in the future, even if their requirements change, without disruption to supply or service.

- It provides staff in registered organisations with a degree of confidence that can only come from knowing that if they carry out their tasks as they have been trained, others will do their part similarly and the customer's requirements will be met consistently, even if those requirements are changed from time to time;

- There is a considerable benefit to management in: reduction of supervision, reduction of time spent sorting out unnecessary problems with customers, both internally and externally; and the provision of a consistent level of operation that enables more effective planning.

A quality management system should be seen more as concerning the management of an organisation and the way that it manages its processes, rather than the quality of what it delivers. If an organisation is managed in an effective, people and process-oriented way, quality will always be delivered in terms of meeting the customers requirements right first time, now and in the future, and all resource's will be dedicated to continuous improvement, i.e. always finding a better way.

ESTABLISHING A QUALITY MANAGEMENT SYSTEM

Most organisations attempting to create a reproducible quality management system create a bureaucratic maze in their attempts to make what they do, based on a traditional management structure, fit the international standard, particularly in terms of *control*. Without a commitment to the fundamentals of total quality management, especially customer–supplier focus, business process orientation, and listening and valuing the voice of the operator of the processes, any attempt to create an effective quality management system which meets the rigorous requirements of the international standard will be difficult and labour intensive to maintain.

The most effective approach to establishing a working, living, effective quality management system is one that uses each individual in establishing exactly what is done within the environment creator processes of the world class organisation as a framework for the total system.

Management activities, tools, continuous improvement activities, and the initiators, creators and sustainers of the world class model all form part of a quality management system. There is always a temptation for organisations which have a registered system to try to operate both the quality management system and their systems for implementing a total quality culture and world class performance, as separate systems. This creates bureaucracy when in fact the two systems should be integrated and operated as one as early as possible. To do this, we need a basic framework against which to develop a system. In most organisations, it is better to consider each major process individually, as a separate quality management system in its own right. Each process needs to be managed in a way which individually would meet the requirements of the international standard. In order to have a framework against which to develop a system to manage our processes and at the same time take account of the requirements of the standard, consider the standard set out in Figure 14.1. Here we see the management requirements and the system requirements set at the top of the structure. This is where the strategic direction comes from. If

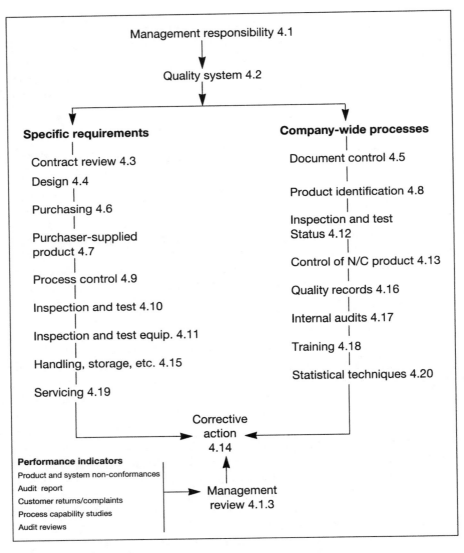

Fig 14.1 Quality system

a good, clear mission has been set in place and communicated correctly to all employees, each process will have its own mission and goals (especially if team purpose analysis is widely used, as seen in chapter 12). Thereafter each process or function should consider first of all the needs of the cross-functional quality management activities which all processes must carry out, together with the special requirements which only certain processes need to consider.

These are linked by the corrective and preventive actions used to maintain and improve the quality of the process performance.

Finally this model is supported on, and by, the management review which itself is fed by the goal-driven measures of process activity and performance.

A quality management system developed against this framework and based on the foundations of total quality management and in a world class environment should produce a system which is easy to maintain and which works dynamically. In Figure 14.2, the requirements and processes of initiating, creating and sustaining a world class organisation are related to the equivalent requirements within ISO 9001.

Consider where you are in terms of the activities of the world class model in chapter 1 and their integration into your quality management system:

- *Can you integrate world class model activities easily?*
- *Will they enhance your systems without losing their power?*
- *Can you rework your quality management system along these guidelines?*

It can be clearly seen from Figure 14.2 that by the effective implementation of the systems and cultural changes required to develop world class performance, an organisation can easily meet and exceed the requirements of ISO 9000.

Often as an organisation develops its sense of empowerment and excellent internal communications systems, some of the requirements of the standard are so automatic that they can become forgotten to the conscious mind. This can cause problems with interpretation, especially with less-flexible, third party auditors. Whilst the spirit of a world class organisation is incorporated within the accompanying documents of the standard, the standard itself is still very stiff and does not recognise the level of empowerment and communication that can exist without affecting the quality of the product or the service.

It has been said before that total quality management cannot exist without a system to manage its processes that is at least a match to ISO 9000. It is also true to say that an organisation cannot aspire to meet the international standard completely unless it embraces some if not all of the foundations of total quality management. For a world class organisation the truth in that statement is even more clear, and some of the additional disciplines which result from maintaining registration, through regular external audits and assessment, ensure that the organisation stays world class.

The world class model	ISO 9000 system requirements
Leadership and Direction	**4.1 Management Responsibility**
Every world class organisation has a real, living mission statement which is understood by and is available to everyone in the organisation.	Management with executive responsibility shall define and document its policy for quality including objectives for quality and its commitment to quality.
The achievement of the mission is described in terms of the attainment of strategic goals, to with are attached key performance measures.	The quality policy shall be relevant to the organisational goals and expectations and needs of the customers. They shall ensure that this policy is understood, implemented and maintained at all levels of the organisation.
Key process improvements are identified and teams established to carry through the improvements.	
The mission, goals, performance measures and improvement targets are cascaded through the organisation in order to provide everyone with personal goals for the activities they perform at every level.	Responsibility and authority and the interrelationship of personnel is clearly defined and documented, particularly for those who need organisational freedom and authority to initiate and implement corrective and preventive action and maintain the continuous improvement process.
Performance, future strategic requirements, goals and improvement requirements are reviewed regularly and necessary changes made. At least annually.	Provide adequate, trained personnel to perform all tasks.
	Provide a manager with executive responsibility with defined authority for ensuring that the quality policy is carried through.
	The senior team shall carry out a review of the quality system at defined intervals to ensure that it continues to be appropriate and effective in meeting the requirements of the International Standard, the customers and the stated quality policy and business objectives.
Process management systems	**4.2 Quality system**
One of management's visible activities within a world class organisation	Organisations shall establish and maintain a documented quality

Fig 14.2 Comparisons between the requirements of ISO and a world class organisation

The world class model	ISO 9000 system requirements
which creates and sustains the culture is to establish systems to manage the processes across the functional boundaries through process mapping and agreeing a single method of execution.	system as a means of ensuring that the product or service conforms to specified requirements. They shall establish a quality manual which defines the structure of the system and how it meets the international standard.
Agreeing the specification of the requirements of the process in terms of its inputs and activities and the establishment of key measures of performance.	Procedures shall be documented consistent with stated policies and the international standard. The system and its procedures will be effectively implemented.
Customer focus	
The foundation of a world class oganisation is to be truly customer-focused, both internal and external, continually monitoring the quality of the service provided.	How quality requirements will be met will be defined and documented in quality plans.
Senior managers should regularly involve themselves at the customer interface to both verify and experience the quality of service provided.	**4.3 Contract review**
	Customers' requirements shall be documented and agreed and reviewed to ensure they can be met.
All aspects of the business must be customer friendly and easy to use.	Differences between order requirements and agreed supply and capability of supplier to provide will be resolved.
Customer requirements must be adequately researched and their requirements must be at the centre of all meetings and business decisions.	Where contracts or orders are amended there shall be systems to ensure that changes to requirements are correctly transferred to the functions in the organisation concerned.
Internally customer–supplier agreements (CSA) are a means of ensuring requirements are documented.	**4.4 Design, control**
	This specialised requirement of the standard applies to organisations which provide products and services especially enveloped to meet the specific requirements of the customer and incorporate all of the requirements of the standard in what amounts to a special form of contract review.

Fig 14.2 contd

The world class model	ISO 9000 system requirements
Communication and ownership of change A major *sustainer* of the world class culture is a formal system to ensure the effective and timely communication of change within the organisation. Part of the responsibility of an improvement, or problem-solving, team is to make the necessary changes in process maps and documentation which result from improvements and changes they have implemented. They are also responsible for the identification of necessary training and its effective implementation.	**4.5 Document and data control** The organisation shall establish and maintain procedures to control all documents and data that relate to the International Standard including, to the extent applicable, documents of external origin such as standards, group instructions (if part of a group of organisations with some central control) and customer drawings.
Customer–supplier, chains A fundamental process within a world class organisation is to ensure the integrity of the customer–supplier chain and to agree quality requirements and the methods by which they will be achieved consistently even when requirements change. Partnerships with suppliers are given equal importance with partnerships with customers.	**4.6 Purchasing** The organisation shall have systems and procedures to ensure purchased product (or services) conform to specified requirements. They will evaluate and select suppliers on the basis of their ability to consistently meet those requirements. Clearly define their requirements and verify the quality capability of the supplier.
Behaviour A key environment creator is agreed codes of behaviour and customer focused-behaviour leads automatically to treating items provided by any outside source as if they belonged to the organisation itself and even the individuals within the organisation.	**4.7 Control of customer-supplied product** Organisations will have systems to identify separately product supplied by the customer and treat it with the same degree of care as the organisation's own product.

Fig 14.2 contd

The world class model	ISO 9000 system requirements
Process management, systems Part of any workable system must permit the unique identification of any element in order to be able to trace the system through and collect data about the process, product and service should anything go wrong. Agreeing how processes should be executed in a common way, training everyone involved to understand the processes they are asked to carry out and having a common code of behaviour in terms of monitoring, measuring and ownership of the process. **Customer–supplier chains** Part of establishing chains between customers and suppliers, the processes of the organisation is a change from an inspection culture (checking at the end of the activity to ask the question 'have we done it correctly this time?') to a culture of prevention, (checking throughout the process that the activity continues to meet specified requirements). This change establishes a culture of monitoring processes continuously. As processes are mapped, the prevention culture is built into the processes.	**4.8 Product identification and traceability** Where appropriate an organisation will provide documented systems for identifying the product (or service) from receipt and during all stages of operation to delivery and installation. The identification shall be unique. **4.9 Process control** An organisation shall identify and plan the production, installation and servicing processes which directly affect quality and shall ensure that these processes are carried out under controlled conditions. **4.10 Inspection and testing** The organisation shall have documented systems and procedures to verify that specified requirements are met. These will cover: – receiving; – in-process inspection and testing; – final inspection and testing; – maintenance of test and inspection records. **4.11 Control of inspection and test equipment** The organisation shall have systems and procedures to control, maintain and calibrate inspection, test and measuring equipment. Where test software or comparative references are used they shall be checked to prove their capability.

Fig 14.2 contd

The world class model	ISO 9000 system requirements
Communication	**4.12 Inspection and test status**
Through the wide application of CSAs and team purpose analysis systems of communicating the status of processes can be established and the behaviour of consistently maintaining the systems agreed.	Suitable means will be established which indicate the inspection and test status of the product or service throughout its cycle. Particularly where the products of activities are non-conforming.
	4.13 Control of non-conforming product
	Documented systems shall be established and maintained to ensure that non-conforming product is identified, segregated and prevented from unintentional use.
	This control shall provide for identification, documentation, evaluation, segregation, disposition and notification to the functions concerned.
Co-ordinated continuous improvement and empowerment through the use of project teams	**4.14 Corrective and preventive action**
In a world class organisation, where the culture is to form a team around a problem to determine the root cause and eliminate it through a systematic process based on the Deming cycle for continuous improvement, effective corrective action is established and implemented by the individuals carrying out the processes.	An organisation shall establish and maintain procedures for implementing corrective and preventive action.
	Any corrective or preventive action taken to eliminate the causes of actual or potential non-conformities shall be of a degree appropriate to the magnitude of the problems and commensurate with the risks encountered.
A world class organisation will have a 'top down' approach to making key improvements to prevent non-conformity in specific areas related to the business plan. These 'top down'	The organisation shall implement and record any changes to the documented procedures resulting

Fig 14.2 contd

The world class model	ISO 9000 system requirements
teams cascade the improvement and preventive actions throughout the organisation to all areas. A robust system for the collection of improvement ideas and converting them into action improves the internal and external service level.	from the corrective or preventive actions. Areas covered shall include: ● handling of customer complaints; ● investigation of root causes; ● determination of the corrective action required to eliminate causes; ● putting in place of controls to ensure effectiveness and non recurrence; ● use of appropriate measurement and data to monitor process to prevent non-conformities occurring; ● effective problem-solving.
Customer–supplier chains The establishment of customer supplier awareness, again through the effective use of CSA and TPA, all operational matters are documented and monitored to ensure continuance to meet requirements and change where needed to meet changed requirements.	**4.15 Handling, storage, packaging, preservation and delivery** Procedures shall be established for the handling (to prevent damage), storage (to prevent and detect deterioration), packaging and marking (to ensure continuing conformance to specification), preservation (and where appropriate segregation), delivery (including protection during transport and timely delivery).
Goal-driven measurement In establishing the responsibilities and reporting of the cascade of key performance measures, formal requirements for the collection, referencing, storage and accessing of information will be agreed and documented.	**4.16 Control of quality records** Systems must be established to identify, collect, file, store, index, access, maintain and dispose of quality records.
Performance appraisal and regular review When a world class organisation has cascaded process ownership and	**4.17 Internal quality audits** The organisation shall establish and maintain documented procedures for planning and implementing internal

Fig 14.2 contd

The world class model	ISO 9000 system requirements
responsibilities to every one and established levels of individual performance these are monitored continuously.	quality audits to verify whether quality activities and related results comply with planned arrangements and to determine the effectiveness of the quality system.
Each individual and process are appraised as often as is necessary to maintain peak performance. Corrective action and improvement goals are established to eliminate variation and shortfall in achieving established goals.	The management personnel responsible or the area where non-conformances are determined shall take timely corrective action on deficiencies found during audits.
Annual reviews of performance are conducted during the establishment of future performance targets for the organisation as a whole.	Follow-up audit activity shall verify and record the implementation and effectiveness of corrective action taken.
	Results of audits are used in management, reviews.
Training	**4.18 Training**
A world class organisation has a highly developed training culture. People are seen as the major asset which makes the organisation unique.	The organisation shall establish and maintain documented procedures for identifying the training needs and pro- viding the training of all personnel performing activities affecting quality.
They are committed to their continuous development, a major element of which is training.	Personnel performing specific tasks shall be qualified on the basis of appropriate education, training and/or experience as required. Appropriate record of training shall be maintained.
It is recognised that training requirements change as processes develop and change and that part of the input to any successful process is the skill of the individual performing that process.	
Customer focus	**4.19 Servicing**
The world class organisation is truly customer-focused and thus will be alert to all requirements both during provision of the product or service and afterwards.	Where servicing is specified as a customer requirement either by contract or by inference of the type of product or service provided, systems shall be established for the

Fig 14.2 contd

The world class model	ISO 9000 system requirements
	performance, verification and reporting as for other processes.
Business processes	**4.20 Statistical techniques**
During the establishment of documented processes within a world class organisation, measurement of their capability and regular monitoring methods will be established as a matter of course.	The organisation shall establish the need for statistical techniques in establishing, controlling and verifying capability and product characteristics.
	Where the need is established, procedures for carrying out the statistical application will be documented.

Fig 14.2 contd

15

Benchmarking

Establishing a world class organisation is one thing, but keeping up with an ever-changing world is quite another

- **What is benchmarking?**
- **Using benchmarking for continuous improvement**
- **Getting started with benchmarking**
- **A systematic model for carrying out benchmarking**

INTRODUCTION

The dictionary definition of benchmarking is 'the surveyors mark ... of previously determined position ... and used as a reference point,' or, 'a standard by which something can be measured or judged'. But what do *We* understand as benchmarking in the continuous improvement sense? Here are two more definitions:

- *It is the process of learning from the best in order to become the best and stay the best.*
- *The measurement of business performance against the best of the best through continuous effort of constantly reviewing process, practice and method.*

True benchmarking is process benchmarking, a structured approach to being the best ... of the best.

Benchmarking can be strategic or organisational. It is a team activity involving the process owner and a team with a clear brief. To be successful, process benchmarking requires a considerable amount of setting up and research time.

Traditionally, we look at improvements in terms of small percentage increases. Yet there is a saying that goes something like this, '... do not mistake the edge of the rut you are in for the true horizon'. By accepting our current performance and accepting small steps to improving that performance, *we* are, mistaking the edge of the rut for the horizon. Most organisations are surprised when they discover that particular process performance in the best of the best, both inside and outside their industry, is often many times better than their own. Gaps of 50 per cent and more in performance, quality and financial terms are not unusual. Bridging that gap requires much more than incremental increases because people who are achieving the best performance are usually those who are also continuously improving.

THREE PRINCIPLE DRIVERS

There are three principle drivers in process benchmarking. They are:

- *Global competition* you must match or exceed the best practice or you won't survive. As the globe continues to shrink in time and space, forward-thinking organisations across the world are accepting that they must match or exceed the best practices of even far-flung competitors, often a realisation from sad experience.

- *Quality awards* there are now quality awards in Europe as well as in the USA and they all require benchmarking as a principle foundation. For example, the Malcolm Baldridge Quality Award in the USA requires applicants to demonstrate competitive analysis and benchmarking in 510 of the 1000 points it contains. Non-benchmarkers need not apply.

- *Breakthrough improvements* Organisations are now realising that to manage the gap between their performance and that of the best of the best requires more than just steady continuous improvement. It requires the sort of improvements that come from breakthrough thinking. Large improvements are often required just to catch up and these can only come from unblinkered, free-thinking people, organised in teams to maximise resources. Continuous improvement in small incremental steps is still required, as are capability studies once a breakthrough is achieved in order to gain control of the new process

FACT OR FAD

It would be easy to think that benchmarking is destined as many other management 'fads' to end up with RIP (retired improvement programme) etched on its tombstone. However, such is the importance of getting out of the rut and seeing the real horizon that benchmarking coupled with a successful total quality management programme is the only way to survive in a global competitive world. Benchmarking is not new. Its origins can be traced back to 607 AD when the Japanese sent teams to China to study the reasons for the successes of the Sui-Dynasty. It is recorded again in the 1800s when during the Meiji Restoration the Japanese again sent teams out around the world to study the best. The Japanese still do it today, but this time to check that someone else hasn't found a better way.

PROCESS BENCHMARKING

Process benchmarking is the continuous comparison of your key processes with the best (domestic and foreign) inside and outside your industry. Benchmarking itself is the process of learning from the best in order to become and stay the best. It is the measurement of business performance against the best of the best, through a continuous effort of constantly reviewing processes, practices and methods. Benchmarking moves us on from: 'Lets improve our performance by x per cent upon current performance,' to 'Let's find out and achieve of the performance of the best of the breed.'

Benchmarking is defined by the Royal Mail as:

'A structured process of learning from the practices of others, internally or externally, who are the leaders in a field or with whom legitimate comparisons can be made.'

To carry out this structured process comprises three steps:

- Learning how others do the process.
- Adapting it to your own organisation.
- Taking action that meets or exceeds the best.

Process benchmarking was really pioneered in the late 1970s in the USA when Xerox, seeing its market share plummeting as a result of Japanese competition and the expiry of design copyright, was forced to reconsider future strategy. Not only were the Japanese competing, but they were selling copiers for less than it cost Xerox to make them. The company was were faced with some stark choices: seek protection, or go for drastic cost reduction measures and down-sizing.

Xerox chose another route. It took benchmarks against the Japanese and learned what processes the Japanese used to be more competitive. Xerox copied and adapted them to meet its own situation and as a result of ten years of hard work, it has survived. Xerox achieved ISO 9001 registration in all of its operations and in 1992 was declared the first recipient of the European Foundation for Quality Management Award. Xerox now uses benchmarking as part of its business process.

This story can be read in the book *Benchmarking* by Robert Camp of Xerox and it details how Xerox benchmarked their 'order entry' process with L L Bean, a specialist mail-order company, because it was the best in its industry. Now companies like AT&T, IBM, ICL, Marks & Spencer, Motorola and many others use benchmarking throughout their businesses as a standard way or operating.

BENCHMARKING MYTHS

It is a mistake to consider that benchmarking is 'competitive analysis'. This latter form of analysis is the comparison of yourself to competitors in your industry. It is largely used for market share, financial measures, competitive strategies and the like. It leads to incremental improvements attitudes and whilst useful at broadening strategy planning, it does nothing to aid breakthrough thinking.

One example of a breakthrough generated by a company outside a specific industry comes from looking at ICL. This computer company wanted to improve its distribution system and found the best comparison in retailer in Marks & Spencer. When Motorola was trying to speed up its delivery process of cellular phones, it paid a visit to Domino's Pizza and Federal Express. When an ammunition manufacturer wanted to make shell cases shinier, it found breakthrough ideas by checking with a lipstick tube manufacturer. When IBM wanted to improve its manufacturing process, it visited Toyota. The latter probably ensured the survival of IBM's Portsmouth UK plant.

Some say *benchmarking is copying*. To some extent this is true. It certainly involves observing and learning from the best practices of others, but if you try and copy their practices exactly it rarely works. Things are seldom the same between organisations. Structure, resource, tradition, culture and so on differ and so to try and copy methods and fit them into your own is a recipe for disaster. Practices must be learned and adapted to fit your situation. At the same time you must try and improve on them otherwise you will continually be in a catch-up cycle. To succeed in benchmarking you must exceed the lessons you learn and accomplish higher goals than those you have seen established.

Benchmarking is often thought of *only in terms of numbers* i.e. comparisons in terms of time, cost and quality. While such numerical comparisons are useful in demonstrating the size of the gap between your performance and the best of the best, it is more important to discover how they obtained those numbers, what measurements they took and look at the processes behind the results that are being achieved.

There is a broad assumption that benchmarking *only applies to manufacturing*. Whilst it is extremely useful in manufacturing, it applies to everything: sales, maintenance, invoicing, purchasing, customer service and systems. In the same way benchmarking equally applies to education, health, defence and government.

Many people are put off initially with thoughts that *competitors won't share*. It is true that direct competitors won't (and shouldn't) share their most competitive secrets. This still leaves a large area where competitors will share and this is well proven, otherwise benchmarking couldn't exist. Under US anti-trust laws, organisations are legally encouraged to share, providing they agree up-front to the areas to be covered and agree to adhere to the information that will be exchanged. Many companies are realising that they must co-operate or be uncompetitive. If they are to learn from others, they must learn to share.

Fig 15.1 gives a model for benchmarking. Also, there is an agreed code of conduct for benchmarking, provided by the International Benchmarking Clearing.

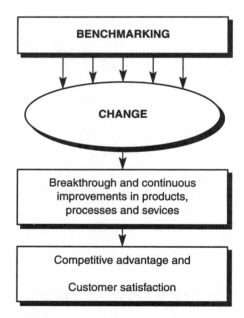

Fig 15.1 The benchmarking process

THE FIVE MUSTS

The essential elements of successful benchmarking are as follows:

- *Senior management must support the benchmarking process* As with all other quality activities, lip service is not enough. Action and participation are the key words. They should be amongst the first to be trained in benchmarking. Up to two days of training should be a minimum and they should participate in the early benchmarking studies as full members of the team and go on visits to other firms.

- *Benchmarking must be part of organisational strategy* A fundamental question in strategic thinking is: 'What does it take to win in this business?'

Benchmarking helps to answer that question and the answer is part of both strategy development and benchmark planning. It requires thinking correctly about what customers want, understanding the critical success factors of the business and the key processes required to achieve them. The very same requirements of a successful total quality programme.

At companies such as B P, Esso, Xerox and Motorola, to name but a few, no major investment, no major project, no major strategy is undertaken without first asking the question: 'Did you benchmark this and what did it tell you?'

Organisational strategy must be customer-focused through its critical success factors.

- *Benchmarking must be a team activity* Benchmarking cannot be done by process owners alone, a team approach is vital. This brings all the benefits that teams bring to problem-solving, process improvement, etc, and avoids uninvolved process owners rejecting the benchmarking information because 'you're comparing apples with oranges', 'we're different', 'it can't work here'.

- *Benchmarking must be planned, organised and managed* Benchmarking, like all other TQM activities and TQM itself, can be launched with noise and enthusiasm, but will die unless it is planned, organised and managed well. Organisation for benchmarking will vary considerably between companies because each has different priorities, key objectives and critical success factors. It is important, as with all TQM activities, to have a benchmarking 'tsar', a banner carrier. Some organisations who are well into benchmarking have set up a department with a small staff to co-ordinate benchmarking activities. Benchmarking must be built into managers' objectives and process owners' performance responsibilities.

Benchmarking must appear appropriate to business goals. Outputs must be measured and monitored just like other important activities.

- *You must understand your own process* Probably the single most common mistake in benchmarking is to begin benchmarking someone else before you understand your own process. To start, you must map your own processes and analyse them first. You must establish performance measures and collect your own data on failure rates and errors, yields and productivity, etc. You need to know cycle times, return on assets and profit margins. You must understand the product, the market and the results of customer surveys. You need all of this before you benchmark others; otherwise you will become industrial tourists, looking on with an untrained eye.

GETTING STARTED

As we have already demonstrated, the first activities in getting started in benchmarking are awareness training and a good understanding of your own processes, through process mapping and analysis. Then you will be ready for the most critical of the start-up activities, *choosing a process to benchmark*.

As with other quality-oriented activities, actions must be seen to be legitimate in terms of being in harmony with the company's business strategy. It must be appropriate in terms of moving the business on if it is to succeed. Once again, you must consider the critical success factors of the organisation and its continuing success within its industry sector.

Critical success factors (CSFs)

Critical success factors are those characteristics, conditions or variables that, when properly sustained, maintained or managed, will have a direct impact on your customer satisfaction, and hence your own success. It may be a specific outcome, result, service level, or other performance target. CSFs significantly affect the overall competitive position or a company. The real critical success factors are linked with customers values and these tend to put the spotlight on key areas where things must go right if your business is to prosper.

Once you have identified these areas, you need to ask questions such as 'How consistent is our capability in this area?' and 'How repeatable is our capability?', followed by 'With what do we compare consistency and repeatability?' In defining appropriate CSFs for a benchmarking topic the following questions may be of use:

- *Is it critical to achieving customer satisfaction?*
- *Will it make a difference to my customer's ability to succeed?*

- *Is this a true indicator or my organisation's ability to prosper and flourish?*
- *Is this applicable to decisions and changes I need to make or problems I need to solve?*
- *Does it fit with the scope of my operation and is it something for which I am directly responsible?*
- *Is it truly a CSF?*

If you cannot answer *yes* to all of these questions, you probably do not have an appropriate topic for benchmarking. You will need to redefine your topic several times until you can answer yes to all of them.

A SYSTEMATIC MODEL FOR BENCHMARKING

The model described below has four steps. Within those steps it has all the elements you require to carry out a successful benchmarking study. It is not an absolute model and in time you will develop your own, but whatever, the elements required remain the same.

Step 1: planning a study

- Select a process.
- Gain owner's participation.
- Select a team and nominate its leader.
- Identify customers' expectations of process.
- Analyse process flows and make measurements.
- Define process inputs and outputs, resources and controls (process cost model).
- Select success factors to benchmark.
- Determine data collection elements and benchmarking measurements.
- Develop a preliminary questionnaire.

Step 2: collecting data

- Collect internal data.
- Perform secondary research (industry and outside industry).
- Identify benchmark partners.
- Develop a survey or interview guide structure.

- Solicit participation of identified partners.
- Collect preliminary date.
- Conduct site visits.

Step 3: analysing data

- Aggregate data.
- Normalise performance.
- Compare current performance to data.
- Identify gaps and root causes.
- Project performance to planning horizon.
- Develop case studies of best practice.
- Isolate the process enablers.
- Assess adaptability of process enablers.

Step 4: adapting and improving

- Set goals to close, meet and exceed the gap.
- Modify enablers for implementation.
- Gain support for change.
- Develop action plans.
- Communicate the plan.
- Commit resources.
- Implement the plan.
- Monitor and report progress.
- Identify opportunities for benchmarking.
- Re-calibrate the benchmark.

SUMMARY

An anonymous commentator once said 'It is important not to mistake the edge of the rut you are in with the horizon.' In benchmarking, you will be preparing to compare yourself with the best in the class producing similar outputs to yourselves and engaged in similar work with similar critical success factors. The result of this comparison is a quantitative representation of the difference between your performance and the best in class can be considerable. Managing this benchmark gap is the challenge. In preparing for benchmarking it is important to identify a CSF to be benchmarked that is customer-focused. Before visiting benchmark partners you must get to know related process capabilities really well. Remember, benchmarking is a experiential and action-oriented learning process. There will be sceptics along the way. You must be converted to the reality that breakthrough thinking when coupled with continuous improvement can produce world class performance, being **THE BEST OF THE BEST**.

The World Class Organisation
is a Reality

APPENDIX I

Organisational Health Check

Before you can develop a formal plan to change the culture of your organisation, you must determine where the organisation is now. The form below will assist you to carry out a comprehensive health check.

Start by completing the form yourself, then if you feel confident about your employees, ask them to complete it and collate the results. (If your organisation has more than, say, 40 employees, invite a sample of them to complete it, ensuring that a sample is representative of all levels, functions and service time.)

When you have gathered the data, you can consider what the results of your health check are telling you by comparing the results with the longer commentary in Appendix 2. This will help you to establish what you will need to change in order to become a world class organisation.

Organisational goals

	Yes	No
1. Do we have a mission statement or corporate goal?	☐	☐
2. Have we clearly communicated this statement to all staff?	☐	☐
3. Do we have detailed strategies to achieve our mission?	☐	☐
4. Are all staff aware of these strategies?	☐	☐
5. Do we have a formal business plan (at least five years ahead)?	☐	☐
6. Are all staff aware of its aims, objectives and requirements?	☐	☐
7. Do we establish and review non-financial performance measures?	☐	☐
8. Do we set and review key process improvement targets?	☐	☐

Organisation structure

	Yes	No
9. Do we have a clear organisation structure?	☐	☐
10. Does everyone have a clear understanding of their responsibilities?	☐	☐
11. Is it the right structure to help us achieve our mission?	☐	☐

	Yes	No

12. Does the structure permit decisions to be taken at the right level? ☐ ☐

13. Are all our staff aware of were they fit into the overall structure? ☐ ☐

14. Are there any aspects of our current structure which could inhibit the implementation of total quality management? ☐ ☐

Management

15. Do we have an 'open' style of management at all levels? ☐ ☐

16. Are all managers skilled in setting objectives for their area of the business? ☐ ☐

17. Are all managers skilled in conducting effective meetings? ☐ ☐

18. Are all managers skilled in the process of decision-making? ☐ ☐

19. Do all managers practise good interpersonal skills? ☐ ☐

20. Do all managers delegate effectively? ☐ ☐

21. Are all staff aware of the standards of performance expected in their jobs? ☐ ☐

22. Has our organisation achieved a recognised quality standard i.e. ISO 9000, NAMAS, Ford Q101, AQAP? ☐ ☐

23. Are all staff aware of the standards of behaviour expected of them in respect of a total quality commitment? ☐ ☐

24. Are all managers skilled in the areas of:

- Time management? ☐ ☐
- Recruitment and selection interviewing? ☐ ☐
- Performance appraisal? ☐ ☐
- Training, development, coaching and presentation? ☐ ☐

Communication

25. Do we have regular formal communication with staff? ☐ ☐

Yes No

26. Do we have formal systems to ensure the free
flow of key information;

- upwards? ☐ ☐

- downwards? ☐ ☐

- across? ☐ ☐

using:

- consultation committees? ☐ ☐

- briefing groups? ☐ ☐

- business review presentations? ☐ ☐

- company videos? ☐ ☐

- other media? ☐ ☐

27. Do we have the appropriate systems to collect
relevant and accurate information from our
customers/suppliers? ☐ ☐

28. Do we have the appropriate systems to deliver ☐ ☐
relevant and accurate information to our customers/suppliers?

29. Do we have the appropriate systems to deliver ☐ ☐
relevant and accurate information to managers and staff?

30. Do we have any identifiable blockages to the ☐ ☐
flow of information through our organisation?

31. Do we have an organisation newspaper or newsheet? ☐ ☐

Customer orientation

32. Do we conduct regular satisfaction surveys of our

- customers? ☐ ☐

- suppliers? ☐ ☐

- employees? ☐ ☐

33. Do all staff really appreciate the concept of ☐ ☐
**Quality = Meeting customers' requirements
and delighting them?**

Yes No

34. Do all staff understand the concepts of:

- the external customer? ☐ ☐
- the internal customer? ☐ ☐

35. Are *all* staff trained in customer contact skills? ☐ ☐

36. Are problem-solving teams in operation? ☐ ☐

Ownership

37. Do we have the style of management which encourages the concept of a working 'partnership'? ☐ ☐

38. Do we have style of management which encourages 'teamwork' and empowerment? ☐ ☐

39. Do all staff feel psychological ownership of our business objectives? ☐ ☐

40. Do all staff feel a psychological ownership of our business problems? ☐ ☐

41. Do we have the business systems to promote a high performance and high pay environment? ☐ ☐

42. Do we work in an organisational atmosphere of mutual trust? ☐ ☐

Total quality culture

43. Has our organisation attempted to introduce culture change before? ☐ ☐

44. Has the initiative been permanently successful? ☐ ☐

45. Does our organisation have an executive decision-maker co-ordinating the quality initiative actions? ☐ ☐

APPENDIX II

Interpreting The Organisational
Health Check

When you have completed the health check in appendix II yourself, or the collation, consider what it is telling you. When you have all your results to hand, let us consider what there is to learn.

ORGANISATIONAL GOALS

1. Do we have a mission statement or corporate goal?

A mission statement or corporate goal provides a focus for all the efforts that are to be made for change. When defining their mission statement, many companies fail to recognise the crucial importance of adequately defining and then expressing the company's purpose. The senior management team must all *own* the company's mission statement. If they do not, the process is flawed from conception

It is not enough that it be the chief executive's mission statement; it must be owned by the whole management team.

From that mission statement the management derives the key goals for the business and then defines the key measures for each of those goals, the appropriate long-term target and the short term milestones for each measure. These are key drivers in the improvement process. This would appear to be simple and straightforward, but it is a process with which most companies have considerable difficulty.

They have difficulty because they do not identify the goals with sufficient clarity and they do not use the goals and measures decided upon to drive the process forward through the whole company.

Consider the key elements of an organisation's properly-developed mission statement. The mission should contain a clear definition of the core business (or if being prepared at a departmental level, the role or contribution of the unit); demonstrate a long-term view (unless the mission is survival) by describing the main things you intend to achieve, worthwhile needs to be fulfilled; and define what you consider to be your distinctive competence. Its purpose should remain constant despite changes in top management and it should be sufficiently explicit for its eventual accomplishment to be verified.

In documenting the mission it should be contained in about four sentences, more and it loses its impact and usefulness.

Each organisation should, in theory, identify four separate goals. It may express them in a number of ways and it may express one goal as two or three, but in essence there are four goals in every properly-developed mission statement. The focus for these goals should always be:

- customer satisfaction;
- people involvement and development;
- financial performance;
- process improvement.

A company may decide to emphasise or de-emphasise one or two particular goals. For example, a business at the forefront of technology may determine that innovation is so vital that although properly a subset of customer satisfaction and process improvement, it becomes a separately identified goal.

2. Have we clearly communicated this statement to all staff?

There are four tests for a good mission statement, it must be *understandable*, so all who read it should immediately understand the aim; it must be *communicable* to all stakeholders by the staff and managers; it must be *believable* by those who have to achieve it (even the sceptics must believe that it could happen even if they are more likely to talk in terms of 'pigs having wings'). Finally, a mission statement must be *usable* in two senses; first as a signpost to provide clear direction to the decision makers, and second usable as a touchstone to return to when the going has been tough. It can be used to plan a fresh course back to the original mission.

With a mission statement, properly explained to employees and shareholders alike, all those who work for the organisation's success are aligned in the same direction.

3. Do we have detailed strategies to achieve our mission?

In setting down the organisation's mission, all we have done is to say this is where we want to go. We have not said how we are going to get there. By identifying the goals in the four key areas we have outlined the route, but not the methodology.

To create the vision and achieve the mission, a detailed set of strategies must be developed, based on a twin-track approach, giving equal consideration to improving the processes and systems and changing the culture.

Having identified the goals, an action plan is developed for each one, showing how the goal is to be achieved and where improvements in performance are most needed. The actions will clearly link the process of developing a total quality culture and world class performance with the day-to-day needs of the organisation and its short-term plans. To complete the establishment of a strategic plan, other 'enabling' policies must be developed from the mission statement and goals cascade giving clear direction on:

- *Communication* Two-way, up, down and across the organisation, involving everyone, in formal and informal communications and a newsletter.
- *Project management* To maximise the involvement of everyone in the improvement process, by cascading the goals and measures to every part of the business and managing the 'bottom up' opportunities for improvement.
- *Recognition* Formal polices to recognise good performance of all types.
- *Reporting* Reporting organisational measures, progress on the implementation and the improvement efforts in a formal way to the business.
- *Performance appraisal and review* A formal system must be developed.

4. Are all our staff aware of these strategies?

The strategic actions must be capable of being deployed into the heart of the organisation down the management line. To help the strategies come alive, each area should consider its support to the main goals by setting improvement goals of its own and developing its own action plans and measures.

5. Do we have a formal business plan?

Part of the preparation of the vision and mission is to consider the organisation's short-term and long-term needs. To do this, the organisation must have a formal business plan based on strategic aims and objectives for the organisation in terms of operational and financial targets and goals, new markets, products and services development and resource plans to achieve the goals. These will be linked to a formal planning and review cycle wherein typically the, say, five-year plan is extended by a further year and the year two forecast becomes the next year one budget.

Once a total quality culture has been established, the business plans and the plan to be world class become totally integrated, because the approaches use the same methodologies. It is simply the thought processes that have to become one.

6. Are all staff aware of its aims, objectives and requirements?

If everyone is to have the same objective, they must all have the same level of information and understanding. World class organisations keep all their employees appraised of long and short-term aims and objectives. They share with them vital market and competitive information in a partnership. No more are the organisation's plans 'top secret', owned only by the chosen few who put them together.

ORGANISATIONAL STRUCTURE

7. Do we establish and review non-financial performance measures?

In addition to the action plans, is necessary to allocate appropriate measures to each goal. The effective use of non-financial measurement, as well as financial, to achieve strategic objectives is one of the fundamental messages within any successful total quality programme. Measurement has traditionally been used across business as a reporting tool or as a control mechanism. Only in some areas has the use of non-financial data as a driver for improved performance become established, most commonly in manufacturing. Even in these areas it can be developed as a 'bottom up' process with measurement being focused on functional repeated activities.

In a world class organisation, measurement's role is changed. It becomes active in the strategic process, a driver of behavioural and process change. For it to play this role, it is necessary that key measures are allocated clearly to each company goal and communicated throughout the company. By definition those key measures have to be limited in number – no-one can manage themselves by a hundred measures – and must be focused upon essential performance elements of the company. The key measures must be limited in number, although below every key measure other measures may exist.

Consider the example of *customer satisfaction* as a *goal*. The identification of the measures is reasonably clear. What is it that customers require of a supplier? First, they require delivery of a complete product or service in a timely manner. Therefore the company should measure its delivery performance in these terms. Customers also require defect-free products. Therefore each company should measure its performance in the supply of defect-free product. Customers also want an error-free relationship with the supplier. Therefore, the appropriate measure of error content must be identified, it may be credit notes for example.

In addition to these specific measures, it is necessary to measure customer satisfaction in a more general sense. Regular and frequent customer surveys provide an appropriate measure.

Key measures for *people involvement and development* will relate to the effectiveness of communication, the availability and effectiveness of training, appraisal and development opportunities and again there will need to be a satisfaction survey.

Process improvement is a more difficult area in which to identify appropriate key measures, but they do exist and should be measured by:

- cycle time;
- waste of materials;
- machine down-time, under-utilised capacity, people waste;
- productivity.

The measurement of *financial performance* means identifying key measures from the large number that exist. Some, such as return on capital employed and overheads are obvious. Others are less obvious and may well be of a different nature in different organisations. It is essential that each management team identify for its organisation the key goals and measures. The foremost management discipline required when implementing a world class programme is to translate these key goals and measures into improved performance.

8. Do we set and review key process improvement targets?

In developing a strategy for a world class operation, a number of key areas for improvement action will be identified. The question always arises, how much improvement do we need?

To become world class, your processes must be the best. You therefore need to set targets for improving those key processes upon which you will be measured. The improvements are never a step change, so you may set a target that you do not expect to hit for two to three years. However, along the way you need milestones that will show you are moving towards your target at the right rate.

9. Do we have a clear organisation structure?

It is particularly true of smaller organisations, or those in the midst of major change, that the organisation structure is unclear. Functional responsibilities become grey and organisational 'black holes' appear where information, requirements and quality ownership can disappear without trace. Even during the implementation of the programme of change, organisation structure must be clear. You may create a dual structure for a short while to facilitate the changes, where you have one structure for business as usual and one superimposed on it to manage the implementation of change, but using wherever possible the main structure.

10. Does everyone have a clear understanding of their responsibilities?

If the main foundation of achieving world class performance is to be customer–supplier chains, then everyone must have a clear understanding of their functional and quality responsibilities. This can be achieved in part through good job descriptions, with training and skill requirements clearly defined. However, to meet the needs of the internal customer and provide a better understanding of individuals responsibilities, agreements may be used to augment job descriptions, both at functional and individual levels.

11. Is it the right structure to help us achieve our mission?

When considering the organisation structure earlier, the need to have two structures in order to manage the initial changes is a good pointer to the structure not being sufficiently well developed for the eventual accomplishment of the mission. Careful consideration of structure is important. Structures closely based on the operational processes with short communication chains have proved more successful in achieving world class status. If changes are required, do not shy away from this. It is important to confront this issue. Take care to ensure that it is seen as a short-term necessity, not a long-term aim, by discussing the issue widely. Implement the necessary changes early.

12. Does the structure permit decisions to be taken at the right level?

Are managers and employees truly empowered? Can they take the decisions that affect their areas of responsibility?

Structures based on traditional functionality force many day-to-day decisions to be taken at too high a level. This leads to frustration on the part of the employees at all levels. Structures based on processes rather than functions, using natural work teams who are empowered to take decisions on matters affecting their areas of responsibility force decisions to be taken at the right levels.

13. Are all staff aware of were they fit into the structure?

Education and awareness of how the operational processes link helps to heighten individual awareness of role and responsibilities within the organisation. This can be best achieved through team purpose or departmental purpose analysis and process mapping. World class organisations as part of their commitment to continuous improvement regularly carry these out. This can be done at departmental or unit level or by the natural work teams.

The process helps the group to: define its purpose and align it to the business strategies and goals; define the requirements and working relationships with its customers and suppliers; identify what is currently being done by the group and if it meets the requirements of its customers and suppliers, and identifies potential improvement opportunities. It is carried out in five steps. First, the group considers its role, what it does and what skills it has. Next, how this fits with the declared organisational mission and goals are discussed; Third, the group defines its customers and suppliers for its major activities, what their requirements are and how well these requirements are met. Then, consideration is then given to how time is actually spent and how much of it meets the customer and supplier requirements. Finally the group considers how it can improve what it does.

In this way, 'teams' can focus their activities on the needs of customers. It also ensures that waste is identified and the teams' activities are aligned to the organisation's requirements, thereby understanding fully their role.

14. Are there any aspects of our structure which could inhibit implementation of TQM?

If you have taken the opportunity to have the health check in appendix 1 completed by a wider audience, consider what the rest of the organisation is telling you, and take action to correct it. Communication barriers are the most likely inhibitors of the implementation of change, rather than the structure. These are usually best dealt with by involving all of the functional leaders during the planning process. Give them complete details of what you are trying to accomplish and get them to buy in to the process.

MANAGEMENT STYLE

15. Do we have an 'open' style of management at all levels?

Despite senior management's good intentions, the organisation can still remain a closed society if the efforts are not repeated at departmental and functional level. This can be countered quite easily by senior managers making themselves more visible and accessible. Regular and unannounced visits to all areas (some call it management by walking about), provides up-to-date information on how well good intentions are being cascaded into the organisation and how they are being received. Your visits can also set the tone and level of 'openness'.

16. Are all managers skilled in setting objectives for their area of the business?

If they are not, you will struggle as you try to cascade the mission and goals. You will probably need to coach your managers in the same process you have used to look at the big picture.

17. Are all managers skilled in conducting effective meetings?

These can be a major contributor to the level of communication and sense of progress within a changing culture. Poor meetings give adverse signals and create frustration. All managers should be able to demonstrate effective meetings skills.

18. Are all managers skilled in decision-making?

For an organisation to exhibit world class performance, its decision-making should be common to all. Every employee must be trained to become skilled at using the process. The chosen methodology must be capable of taking account of views from all those affected by the decision, as well as the mission and core objectives of the organisation.

19. Do managers practise good interpersonal skills?

The recognition of the *internal customer* is a keystone to building a world class organisation. This must come from the top. Everyone has internal customers who must be treated with the same level of personal service as the external customer. Managers must practise a high degree of interpersonal skill when handling staff and when dealing with other individuals. They should cultivate a high level of personal service for dealing with their internal customers.

20. Do managers delegate effectively?

No individual is an island in a world class organisation. Day-to-day jobs and responsibilities must be delegated to create the time and space for effective planning for improvement. Managers must be able to delegate effectively if their areas of responsibility are not to show signs of strain under the workload that comes with creating the right environment for cultural change.

Effective delegation means empowerment. It does not mean the abrogation of responsibility. With effective delegation, individuals feel empowered. They have the authority to carry out tasks; they feel responsible for the task, even though the delegating manager still holds ultimate responsibility. Effective delegation requires the identification of the right person to take on the task; giving clear instructions; establishing clear lines of authority and responsibilities; and regular monitoring to ensure the delegation and empowerment is working.

21. Are staff aware of the standards of performance expected in their jobs?

Individuals and departments cannot be expected to perform to their full potential or to achieve the level of internal and external customer satisfaction unless they know precisely what is expected. Without clear, agreed, performance standards, activity cannot be measured. Without measurement improvements cannot take place.

22. Has our organisation achieved a recognised quality standard?

As we all know, acquiring recognition of any particular quality standard can often be as much a mark of what you don't say you do as what you do. However, if you are committed to world class performance, regular external assessment of the systems you have established keeps you up to the mark, stops back-sliding and the infiltration of bad practices.

23. Are staff aware of the standards of behaviour expected of them in respect of a total quality commitment?

Training everyone to understand the concept of internal customers and suppliers is an important element in the initial introduction of the total quality culture and is fundamental to its development. However, the early establishment of the *values, practices* and *behaviour* that will underpin the move to change the culture of the organisation is equally important. This will be achieved by establishing 'role model behaviour' and managers practising it visibly throughout the organisation.

24. Are managers skilled in time management; recruitment and selection interviewing; performance appraisal; training, development, coaching and presentation?

Each of these should be part of any 'role model manager's' profile. Part of the implementation plan should include training in each of these areas.

COMMUNICATION

25. Do we have regular formal communication with staff?

A vital element in the winning of hearts and minds of the staff is *open communication*. It is also vital in winning their trust. You will be changing many things and your staff must *trust* that when they need to know about something they will be informed fully. Such trust is built, again, through senior management action. Establishing *regular*, and *formal*, communication helps to build trust.

26. Do we have formal systems to ensure free flow of key information?

Downwards?

The way you inform employees of business plans, business performance, changes in the market, competition activity, policy developments, successes and failures and, senior management thinking is important. Keeping a regular flow of information from the 'top' to all staff requires well-constructed and controlled systems. The performance of these systems is as important as any of your other business systems and therefore must be measured, monitored and reviewed regularly.

Upwards?

Employees must also feel that senior management will listen to their voice if an environment of involvement and empowerment is to be created and sustained. A system of capturing employee communications and taking them right to the 'top' where a positive response can be developed and cascaded back through the organisation must be developed. It is not sufficient to run a suggestion scheme or a routine forum. Regular facilities for taking communication up through the organisation and responding to it is essential.

Across?

This can be done using consultation committees; briefing groups; business review presentations; company videos and other media.

27. Do we have appropriate systems to collect information from customers and suppliers?

Part of being a *customer-focused* means developing good channels of communication with customers (and suppliers) so that we can review our performance, in terms of meeting their requirements, regularly. Through the same channels we should be able to collect information regarding future changes in customers' (and suppliers') requirements so we can make the necessary changes to our processes and systems to enable us to continue to delight them. Regular, independent surveys of how well we meet their requirements and what other services and/or products they would like to see from us is part of continuous improvement.

28. Do we have appropriate systems to deliver information to our customers and suppliers?

As above.

29. Do we have appropriate systems to deliver information to managers and staff?

Whilst most of the elements for consideration are covered the two preceding items, the senior management in world class organisations will regularly review the information they pass to their managers to ensure it remains relevant, accurate and timely. Always try to beat the grapevine.

30. Do we have any identifiable blockages to the flow of information?

As a critical processes within any organisation, systems for communication and information flow should be the subject of a regular process team review, always analysing the process accurately and probing to identify and eliminate any blockages or potential blockages.

31. Do we have an organisation newspaper or newsheet?

Internal marketing is a vital ingredient in the successful implementation plan. Depending on the individual organisational culture, this may be high or low-profile but it is needed to communicate progress and to provide wider recognition of individual success. If there is already a proven method through the use of a regular newspaper of newsheet, its use should be continued. Where there is none, one should be developed into an organisation-wide organ of recognition, not just for the cultural change programme, at the earliest point.

CUSTOMER ORIENTATION

32. Do we conduct regular satisfaction surveys of customers, suppliers and employees

Regular satisfaction surveys should feature widely in the measurement of progress to change culture to one of total quality.

33. Do staff really appreciate the concept of quality?

Part of this will be addressed by the training described earlier but that should be taken a step further with all employees experiencing the total quality foundations and developing and understanding of the type of organisation that is envisaged in performing at a world class level.

34. Do staff understand the concepts of external and internal customers?

Whilst most employees will readily identify with the *external* customer, they will less readily identify with their *internal* customers. Training will help, but it must be reinforced within the function or area by the regular use of *departmental purpose analysis, team purpose analysis* and routine use of agreements together with suitable performance measurement. These tools are described in chapter 15.

35. Are staff trained in customer contact skills?

When dealing with the *internal* customer it is just as important to use good customer contact skills as it is when dealing with *external* customers. In fact during a period of change, it is often more important. This is equally true when dealing with *suppliers*. They too are customers and the same skills must be demonstrated when dealing with them.

36. Are problem-solving teams in operation?

Many individuals have made a career out of solving problems. Unfortunately, their reputation has often been built on an ability to solve the same problem, fast, over and over again. This means they never solved the problem at all, they are just good a papering over the cracks.

Problem-solving teams bring the brainpower of all those effected by the problem or by the solution together. They find the root cause and eliminate it, replacing the offending process, system, practice or behaviour with something better that has everybody's support. In a world class organisation, the manager no longer solves a problem alone, handing down the answer to those who have to implement the solution. They are all involved in building a solution together.

OWNERSHIP

37. Do we have the style of management which encourages the concept of a working partnership?

The traditional model of enlightened leadership stops short of the style of leadership required by organisations which wish to achieve world class performance. It suggests that the ideal level of freedom for the subordinate is found in *delegation–permitting subordinates to function within defined limits*. Within a total quality culture, managers must build working partnerships with their staff to encourage innovation and feelings of empowerment

38. Do we have the style of management which encourages 'teamwork' and empowerment?

Setting up and managing cross-functional, multi-disciplined teams to solve high-level problems is only one step towards establishing 'teamwork' as part of 'business as usual '. Managers must encourage natural work teams, built around people who normally work together, although not necessarily in the same job. As individuals become more familiar with the tools and techniques of continuous improvement through working in the formal process improvement teams, they will naturally wish to make improvements in their own areas, quietly, less formally. It is an important new role of the manager and supervisor to support such activities and provide coaching to them.

39. Do staff feel psychological ownership of our business objectives?

Share schemes and the like are not necessarily what is needed for individual employees and managers to feel a psychological ownership of the business objectives. They need to have been consulted during the establishment of any business plan and feel that they have been listened to. Participation is the key.

40. Do staff feel a psychological ownership of our business problems?

Again, participation is the key. Keeping staff informed about business successes and failures is important if staff are to take ownership of the bad as well as the good. If they expect to be consulted, involved in developing solutions to problems and development of processes to avoid the problems, they will be interested. Where they are not interested, consider how much they are told and involved with real customer problems.

41. Do we have the systems to promote a high performance and high pay environment?

It is often heard said by employees that one person gets paid more for working less. Reward is seldom equitable with effort. In a world class organisation, the reward structure should reflect how hard individuals work, what they contribute to the wealth creation of the organisation, not necessarily the title or position or how long they have worked for the organisation. Ways must be found to regularly reward the people who consistently give more than 100 per cent. This will need some new thinking; traditional ways don't work.

42. Do we work in an organisational atmosphere of mutual trust?

How close do you still supervise your people including the most senior of your managers? Why do you pay for expensive training if you are still going to do the job yourself? How much do you tell them? Can you trust them with financial information? Market information? Structural change information?

'Train, trust and inform your people and they will reward you many times' is a quotation credited to a manager at Toyota, a truly world class organisation. If people are to commit to never-ending continuous improvement, they will only do it in an atmosphere of mutual trust.

43. Has our organisation attempted to introduce culture change before?

If you have given an affirmative response here, write down a list of all the initiatives you have used. How were they received? Which ones worked best? Why?

44. Has the initiative been permanently successful?

Can you demonstrate that permanent changes have taken place as a result of the initiatives and can you put hard figures on the improvements'. If you have answered yes, then gut feel alone is not enough. Make sure you are not in a fool's paradise.

45. Does our organisation have an executive decision-maker co-ordinating quality initiative actions?

Organisations find considerable benefit in appointing a senior member of the management team to co-ordinate the culture change actions and to act as a senior management facilitator. Typically they would devote at least half of their time in the first year.

If the organisation does not have a strategic business plan, or a statement of objective (corporate goal or mission statement) then these need to be developed in order to provide employees with a common direction and the means of measuring progress.

BIBLIOGRAPHY

Barker Joel Arthur, (1990), *Discovering the Future*, Charthouse International Learning Corporation, Burnsville, MN.

Barker Joel Arthur, (1992), *Future Edge*, Charthouse International Learning Corporation, Burnsville, MN.

Blanchard Kenneth, Zigarmi Patricia, Zigarmi Drea, (1986), *Leadership and the One Minute Manager*, William Collins Sons & Co., Glasgow.

Briggs Myers Isobel, Myers Peter B., (1980) *Gifts Differing*, Consulting Psychologists Press, Inc., Palo Alto, CA.

Camp Robert, (1989), *Benchmarking*, Quality Press, Milwaukee, Wisc.

Crosby Phillip B., (1979), *Quality is Free*, New York: McGraw–Hill Book Company.

Dale Barrie G, Oakland John S. *Quality Improvement Through Standards*, London: Stanley Thornes (Publishers) Limited.

Deming Walter E., (1982), *Quality, Productivity, and Competitive Position* MIT Centre for Advanced Engineering Study, Cambridge, Mass.

Deming Walter E., (1986), *Out of a Crisis*, MIT Centre for Advanced Engineering Study, Cambridge, Mass.

Ishikawa Kaoru [translated by David J Lu], (1985), *What is Total Quality Control? – the Japanese Way*. Englewood Cliffs, NJ: Prentice–Hall.

Juran Joseph M., (1979), *Quality control Handbook* 3rd Edition, New York: McGraw–Hill Book Company.

NEDO, (1985) *Quality and Value for Money*, A report to the NEDC by the task force on Quality and Standards, National Economic Development Office, London.

Oakland John S., (1989), *Total Quality Management*, London, Heinemann.

Peters Thomas J., Waterman Robert H. Jr, (1982), *In Search of Excellence*, New York: Harper and Row Publishers.

USEFUL ADDRESSES

Association of Quality Management
Consultants
4 Beyne Road
Olivers Battery
Winchester
Hants. SO22 3JW

Tel: 01962 864394
Fax: 01962 866969

British Association for Psychological Type
Emmaus House
Clifton Hill
Bristol
BS8 4PD

Tel: 01272 466797

British Standards Institute
BSI Quality Assurance
PO Box 375
Milton Keynes
MK14 6LL

Tel: 01908 220908
Fax: 01908 220671

British Quality Foundation
1st Floor,
215, Vauxhall Bridge Road
London
SW1V 1EN

Tel: 0171 963 8000
Fax: 0171 963 8001

Department of Trade and Industry
151 Buckingham Palace Road
London
SW1W 9SS

Tel: 0171 215 1532
Fax: 0171 215 1306

European Foundation for Quality
Management
Avenue des Pleiades, 19
1200 Brussels
Belgium

Tel: (+32) 2 775 3511
Fax: (+32) 2 775 3535

International Benchmarking Clearinghouse
IFS
Wolseley Road
Wolseley Business Park
Kempston
Bedford
MK42 7PW

Tel: 01234 853605
Fax: 01234 854499

Investors in People UK
4th Floor
7–10 Chandos Street,
London
W1M 9DE

Tel: 0171 636 1626
Fax: 1071 636 2386

National Society for Quality through
Teamwork
2 Castle Street
Salisbury
Wilts.
SP1 1BB
(also base for the British Deming
Association)

Tel: 01722 326667
Fax: 01722 331313

Oxford Psychologists Press
Lambourne House
311-321 Banbury Road
Oxford
OX2 7JH

Tel: 01865 510203
Fax: 01865 310368

Warmbrook Consultancy
Ridgeside House
4 Copse Close
Wirksworth
Derbyshire
DE4 4PQ

Tel: 01629 823354
Fax: 01629 823354

For further details on the wider application of the checklists and models described in this book – contact the author, Michael E Joyce on (01629) 823354.

INDEX